*Don't Be a Victim:
Choose Victory!*

# Don't Be a Victim: Choose Victory!

Dealing and Winning in a Fallen World

## Carey Scott O'Neal, Jr.

*Forewords by Timothy Beougher,
Woods Watson, and Dave Hume*

RESOURCE *Publications* • Eugene, Oregon

DON'T BE A VICTIM: CHOOSE VICTORY!
Dealing and Winning in a Fallen World

Copyright © 2021 Carey Scott O'Neal, Jr. All rights reserved. Except for brief quotations in critical publications or reviews, no part of this book may be reproduced in any manner without prior written permission from the publisher. Write: Permissions, Wipf and Stock Publishers, 199 W. 8th Ave., Suite 3, Eugene, OR 97401.

Resource Publications
An Imprint of Wipf and Stock Publishers
199 W. 8th Ave., Suite 3
Eugene, OR 97401

www.wipfandstock.com

PAPERBACK ISBN: 978-1-7252-8781-5
HARDCOVER ISBN: 978-1-7252-8782-2
EBOOK ISBN: 978-1-7252-8783-9

03/04/21

# Contents

*Forewords by Timothy Beougher, Woods Watson, and Dave Hume* | vii
*Introduction* | ix

Day 1: How Did We Get So Victim Focused? | 1
Day 2: America's Founding Fathers Were Victims | 6
    *But with God's Help Escaped That Victim-Status and Became Conquerors*
Day 3: Why I Believe God Is Real, Alive, Active in Our Lives
    and Loves Us All | 11
Day 4: Who and/or What Is the Christian God? | 16
Day 5: You Are Not Alone—Ever | 23
Day 6: Are Heaven and Hell Real Places? | 26
Day 7: Dealing with Survivor's Guilt | 30
Day 8: God Has a Plan for Our Lives | 35
    *The Path to a Joyful and Peaceful Existence*
Day 9: Dealing with Being Prideful | 39
Day 10: Delighting in Our Weaknesses | 44
Day 11: Dealing with Being Brokenhearted | 48
Day 12: Dealing with Depression | 55
Day 13: Dealing with Loneliness and Isolation | 62
Day 14: Dealing with Shunning Someone or Being Shunned | 66
Day 15: Understanding Repentance and Forgiveness | 71
Day 16: Forgiving Yourself | 77
Day 17: Dealing with Anger | 80
Day 18: Controlling My Tongue | 84
    *Grace-vs-Condemnation*

Day 19: Dealing with Guilt | 88
Day 20: Dealing with Lack of Control | 91
Day 21: Being Able to Endure | 93
Day 22: Dealing with Worry | 96
Day 23: Dealing with Fear of Death | 99
Day 24: Dealing with Fear during Unsettling Times | 101
Day 25: Dealing with Our Failures | 104
Day 26: Dealing with Envy/Covetousness | 107
Day 27: God Promises Us Hope through Jesus | 109
Day 28: Is Illness/Suffering "Punishment" from God? | 112
Day 29: Who or What Is Your God? | 118
Day 30: Where Your Treasure Is, There Your Heart Will Be . . . | 122
Day 31: When I Die . . . | 125
Day 32: Hearing What God Has to Say to Us | 128
Day 33: God's Grace Is Sufficient in Every Situation | 132
Day 34: God Is Faithful | 136
Day 35: Why Obey God? | 139
Day 36: The Holy Spirit . . . Who Is He? | 142
Day 37: Is Worshipping God Relevant in Today's World? | 146
Day 38: Finding Joy and Peace through Worship | 151
Day 39: Abiding with Christ | 154
Day 40: Press On | 157

*Conclusion* | 160

# Forewords

CHARLES HADDON SPURGEON, THE renowned England Baptist preacher, once remarked that people should divide their libraries into two sections: biographies and everything else. Spurgeon was a great lover of all types of books, but he understood the power of biography to challenge and inspire. While technically a "devotional" and not a "biography," my friend Scott O'Neal uses instances throughout his life to demonstrate the love and faithfulness of God. Scott saturates this book with Scripture and prayer. I am confident that Scott's tracing of his journey on the walk of faith will inspire your journey as well. It has done so for me.

Blessings,

**Timothy K. Beougher**
B.S., Th.M, Ph.D. Associate Dean, Billy Graham School of Missions, Evangelism and Ministry; Billy Graham Professor of Evangelism and Ministry; Billy Graham Professor of Evangelism and Church Growth (1996); Senior Pastor, West Broadway Baptist Church, Louisville, KY

• • •

SCOTT O'NEAL CARES ABOUT people. His heart is to help others. Using a combination of personal life experiences and biblical truths, Scott has presented credible helps to people who are in need. His insights flow from his rigorous self-evaluation informed by Christian teaching. He has provided many pathways to assist others to come to wholeness.

Recently I heard Dr. Tim Jennings, author of the *Aging Brain*, describe what he learned in his research for helping others, who have been negatively affected by unfair, hurtful relational experiences. Dr. Jennings revealed that personal healing came when people moved toward truth, took personal responsibility for their own violations of God's laws, and released the bitterness and hatred they have held against the perpetrators of their pain. Scott's tome reflects this process and I would anticipate would produce similar results.

Scott does not write as an academic theorist but as a fully engaged practitioner. He has written as much from his heart as from his head. His emotions flow through his words. He cares deeply and feel strongly; the reader will benefit from both. The reader will be able to relate easily to his transparent revelations (I do not think I feel secure enough to be this open.) and will sense the full measure of his exhortations. I hope great good for others will come from this. I am confident that Scott's hope and prayer is that it does.

**Dr. J. Woods Watson**
Adults Group Pastor
First Baptist Church First West, West Monroe

• • •

MY FRIEND SCOTT O'NEAL is the author of this book and, at the author's request I read the draft. In this writing the author is drawing primarily on his experience as a sinner, a military aviator, a husband and by the grace of God, a Christian. You will find the author honestly expressing life's difficulties and most impressive is how each chapter ends by expressing the goodness of God by giving glory to God. Knowing the author personally and as a current brother in Christ (I am his Sunday School Teacher and friend), I think you will find this writing intriguing, honest, spiritual, and most importantly Christ centered. I pray you will be inspired and perhaps challenged by this writing. God bless as you read.

**Dave Hume**
Pharmacist (ret'd), Deacon, Outreach Leader, and Sunday School Teacher—West Broadway Baptist Church, Louisville, KY

# Introduction

First, I need to acknowledge the tremendous help that was given to me in the editing of this project by Dr. Timothy Beougher and Dr. Woods Watson. Dr. Beougher is the Associate Dean of the Billy Braham School of Missions, Evangelism, and Ministry, and Professor of Evangelism and Church Growth at the Southern Baptist Theological Seminary in Louisville, KY. Dr. Watson is the Adult Groups, Senior Adults, and Pastoral Care Ministries Pastor at the First Baptist Church in West Monroe, LA. I cannot express my appreciation loud or long enough to acknowledge how grateful I am to them for their time and effort in the editing of this work. It could not have become what it is now without their input, and I want them to know how much I appreciate their assistance.

What is a victim and what does it mean to be a victim? Merriam Webster defines a victim like this: "one that is acted on and usually adversely affected by a force or agent: (2): one that is subjected to oppression, hardship, or mistreatment." Are there real victims in this world? Absolutely there are; some groups of victims are people who are victimized by acts of nature (hurricanes; floods, famines, lightning, etc.), acts of carelessness (drunk drivers, faulty products, bad medicines, etc.), and acts of evil (terrorism,

*Introduction*

bigotry, war, racism, revenge, etc.). Generally, victims are individuals who are harmed by someone or something out of their control.

Because someone is victimized does not mean that they must go through life letting victimization define how they live the rest of their lives. That is a choice every individual must make. I chose, with God's help, to not define my life as a victim. Instead, I chose to overcome the conditions in my life that had victimized me and press on; to become a victor and live my life in the joy of my personal relationship with Jesus Christ, my Savior.

I am no longer suffering with the "victim" syndrome that many of us are battling. I am just a guy who spent over thirty years fighting complexes, self-loathing, feeling persecuted and feeling victimized. But God has brought me through that, and now, I consider myself a VICTOR, not a VICTIM!

How did I accomplish this? To boil it down simply, it was three basic steps: (1) I trusted God to keep His word as promised in Jeremiah 29:11 *"For I know the plans I have for you," declares the LORD, "plans to prosper you and not to harm you, plans to give you hope and a future."* (2) I turned control of my life over to God. (3) I followed wherever He led. I still pray and seek God's will for my life every day. I do not make any decisions in my life without seeking God's will and then doing what I feel He is directing me to do. Sometimes those paths are very clearly defined, and sometimes they are not so clear. Then, I go by faith and seeking wise counsel from my wife and other Christians, I want to share with anyone who will read this that I now know that they do not have to live with feeling victimized; they can break out with God's help and become a VICTOR regardless of their race, creed, color, health abilities or disabilities, or economic status in life.

So why write this book? I can assure you the reason is not for the money. If God blesses me enough to let this book be published, I have promised God that I will be donating at least ninety percent (90%) to Christian charities that help the underprivileged and the disabled American veterans. Call it an epiphany, a life lesson, or a compulsion; I am not sure what the best way to describe my motivation.

As a returning soldier from two different deployments to a war zone, I had a difficult time adjusting back to civilian life. I had that "victim" syndrome. I felt my company did me wrong while I was deployed to the Middle East during Operation Desert Storm. I felt my immediate and higher supervisors did not show me the respect I deserved, or even do what the law said they should do for me while deployed. For over five years, I tried everything I could to get out of my current job and transfer to something

*Introduction*

different inside my company, but everything I tried did not pan out, and I became more and more frustrated.

Then, in November of 1996, after what seemed to be the most promising new opportunity failed to work out, I was fuming. On a Thanksgiving family camping trip, I went into the woods and had a real shouting match between God and myself (mostly me doing the shouting!). I was tired of fighting, tired of being angry, and tired of feeling like a victim. The negativity of the situation was affecting me in many ways, depression, frustration, anger, and on my job. I felt broken. I just gave up the fight; I told God that I could not continue like I was going, and I asked Him for forgiveness for my sins, and I asked Him to change my whole attitude. I gave God permission to do whatever He needed to do to heal me from my depressed and angry self. I told Him that I would no longer try to do anything on my own in my life; and I asked Him to take control of my life. I told Him that I would not try to make anything happen with my career but would totally depend on Him if anything was to change. If He did not wish anything to change, I asked Him to give me a better attitude and to give me acceptance of His choices and to help me be happy again.

Two weeks later, out of the blue, my boss called me and asked me if I wanted to move to Pensacola, FL. It was the perfect assignment for me at the time. My new boss was now going to be about six hours away from me in Jacksonville. I was moving into a market where my predecessor had been highly successful for several years and had been promoted. Pensacola was treated almost like a remote location where I was the senior person in job level, with a terrific but highly independent group of technicians, installers, and support personnel who wanted nothing more than to just be left alone and to have things rock along as before. God proved himself to me, and I have given Him control of my life since that date with no regrets!

The ongoing war in Iraq and Afghanistan has created tens of thousands of soldiers coming back from multiple combat tours. I have seen and met a lot of hurting and confused young soldiers who were experiencing much of which I also had experienced. I wanted to help them. But, at the same time, I felt like writing a book like this might also be a cathartic process for me, which it has been. There are literally millions of people who feel victimized by any number of individuals, races, businesses, or governmental bodies. They, too, can hopefully receive enlightenment, encouragement, and healing by realizing they do not need to let those intentionally manipulating, victimizing,

## Introduction

or oppressing them do so. With God's help, they can control their own destinies and be the people and live the life God intends for them to be.

Being a winner in life (and not being a victim!) is a choice believe it or not. The FIRST choice is to seek God for help. He can enable us to be the winners He wants us to be! It is not like a baseball or football game, or a competition between companies for another customer's business. As my pastor, Dr. Timothy K. Beougher said to me, *". . . As I read this paragraph, I am reminded that God calls us to be thermostats (where we control the temperature of our environment), not thermometers (which simply reflect the temperature of our environment)."*

Being a winner in life is deciding whether we let life beat us down and make victims out of us, or whether we decide that whatever ups and downs, hurdles, difficult choices or seemingly impossible situations we find ourselves in, we will find a way to endure, adapt, overcome and be victorious in the struggle to get through this brief time on earth. I choose with God's help to be a winner. I choose to be a thermostat. I choose victory, and hopefully in this book, with Jesus' help, I will be able to encourage others to overcome their victimhood and choose to be a VICTOR!

## Day 1

## How Did We Get So Victim Focused?

> Who shall separate us from the love of Christ? Shall trouble or hardship or persecution or famine or nakedness or danger or sword? As it is written: "For your sake we face death all day long; we are considered as sheep to be slaughtered." No, in all these things we are more than conquerors through him who loved us. For I am convinced that neither death nor life, neither angels nor demons, neither the present nor the future, nor any powers, neither height nor depth, nor anything else in all creation, will be able to separate us from the love of God that is in Christ Jesus our LORD."
>
> ROMANS 8:35–38

ARE THERE REAL VICTIMS in the world today? Absolutely. Today in America, the media and lawyers have created an atmosphere where virtually everybody feels victimized by someone or something, and that in-turn creates resentments and even hatred towards everything and everyone that one feels is making them a victim. What is sad to me as a Christian is the utter denial of people to realize that much of their feelings of being victimized are either created or blown out of proportion by individuals and groups content to allow those feelings to fester and be blown out of proportion. These manipulators are people and groups who literally brainwash people into believing there is "no-way-out" of being a victim except by violence and rebellion against whomever they feel like are their oppressors. The victims are simply being manipulated to further the control and oppression of those who victimize them to further their own positions, power, and wealth. These manipulators create attitudes in the victims of anger and rebellion which inevitably lead to negative consequences. This is one of the cruelest acts of treachery and manipulation of other individuals that can be inflicted by one human on another. In virtually all of history, where humans are manipulated by others, the outcomes of their rebellion have ended up causing more harm to those that were being manipulated than any good from the rebellion.

Simply stated, anger, rebellion, and striking out against those that are manipulating us does no good. Only through prayer, through recognizing how we are being manipulated and not allowing that to happen, and through allowing God to help us help ourselves out of our victimization syndrome can we create a positive outcome for ourselves. It is our choice.

The victim mentality started becoming prevalent in America during the Civil Rights movement of the 1950's and 1960's which rightfully protested the discrimination in this nation towards the negro community. Although the blacks in America had been freed as slaves during the Civil war in the middle of the 1800's, they were still discriminated and looked down upon by non-blacks as "non-equals."

Thanks to courageous leaders in the black community like Dr. Martin Luther King, Jr. and Medgar Evers, the black citizens of America, after enduring persecution and violence against them for standing up for their Constitutional rights, were victorious in their efforts to establish equal rights under the law when in 1964 the Civil Rights Act of 1964 became law. It would have been wonderful if when that law was passed, all of America would have accepted that law and given black Americans that status both legally and morally, but that did not happen. Discrimination reigned on for several decades in which the black community continued to face discrimination, although at times it was disguised or only given token acceptance.

Now, in the twenty-first century, although we still hear the cry of people who still cling to their discriminatory beliefs, America has become much less discriminatory against our black brothers and sisters and most any other minority that one can imagine. The hate and discrimination have surfaced in recent years against homosexuals, transsexuals, bisexuals, pro-abortionists, and in most recent years, the Christians in America. Lawsuits abound against Christians who protest against abortion, who choose not to do business with individuals who violate their religious beliefs, who promote the values of our founders in such areas as disciplining our own children, against school systems which choose to inflict corporal punishment on their children, against displaying religious symbols on government properties, etc.

The American Civil Liberties Union, which started in 1920 has as its stated mission *"to defend and preserve the individual rights and liberties guaranteed to every person in this country by the Constitution and laws of the United States."* In the last forty years, however, the ACLU has taken up the mission of attacking the Constitution and the Bill of Rights in specific areas like the discrimination against homosexuals, atheists, agnostics, abortion activists, as well as continuing their activities against racial and sex discrimination.

All these revolutions in civil rights have generated thousands of "victims" where people feel like they have been discriminated against somehow. Add to that the untold number of lawsuits by plaintiff lawyers looking to generate huge fees by suing businesses where they have people who say they have been "injured" somehow by the products and services companies provide, and we now have a legal system that is drowning in lawsuits which create in people the feelings of being mistreated for any number of reasons.

This victim mentality is one that is destructive and dangerous because it tends to create in people's mind that their physical, mental, or social maladies are always someone else's fault. While certainly there are legitimate cases where individuals are victimized, this mentality and the "sue somebody" mentality are responsible for creating a society that has an attitude of hostility and "it's not my fault" towards those that are the targets for lawyers and the legal system. It gives them an excuse for not having to take responsibilities for their own actions and destinies.

This kind of attitude is not biblical, and it is certainly not the attitude our founding fathers wished to establish when they wrote the Declaration of Independence and the Constitution of the United States of America. For instance, in the preamble to the Constitution, the writers use strong action words when they said "establish" Justice, "ensure" domestic tranquility, "provide" for the common defense, and "secure" the blessings of liberty. These are words with finality and assurance of an action being completed. However, when they talked about the welfare of the population, they used a softer action word," promote," a softer word with an open-ended time frame and undefined action plan.

God created humans with the instinct to search for something in life to fulfill us. The Bible says that mankind was created "in the image of God"

## Don't Be a Victim: Choose Victory!

*(Then God said, "Let us make mankind in our image, in our likeness, so that they may rule over the fish in the sea and the birds in the sky, over the livestock and all the wild animals, and over all the creatures that move along the ground." So God created mankind in his own image, in the image of God he created them; male and female he created them." Genesis 1:26–27).*

Mankind over the centuries has tended to lose sight of the fact that God created us for the purpose of fellowship with Him. Yes, are expected to work and earn our keep in this life, but our work is NOT to be the main purpose for which we live. His intent is for us to work to live, feed our families, and to live out His plan for our lives. That is what He has promised will provide us the most personal *happiness* and gratification for our time here on earth. We were not created to live out our lives pursuing earthly efforts for personal gratification, God created us to live out His plan for our lives pursuing His plan for us to serve and worship Him, relying on his promise that if we do, our lives will be fulfilled beyond our expectations. His promises are plain and truthful when He says:

> "Do not store up for yourselves treasures on earth, where moth and rust destroy, and where thieves break in and steal. But store up for yourselves treasures in heaven, where neither moth nor rust destroys, and where thieves do not break in or steal; for where your treasure is, there your heart will be also." . . . "For this reason I say to you, do not be worried about your life, *as to* what you will eat or what you will drink; nor for your body, *as to* what you will put on. Is not life more than food, and the body more than clothing? Look at the birds of the air, that they do not sow, nor reap nor gather into barns, and yet your heavenly Father feeds them. Are you not worth much more than they? And who of you by being worried can add a single hour to his life? And why are you worried about clothing? Observe how the lilies of the field grow; they do not toil nor do they spin, yet I say to you that not even Solomon in all his glory clothed himself like one of these. But if God so clothes the grass of the field, which is alive today and tomorrow is thrown into the furnace, will He not much more clothe you? You of little faith! Do not worry then, saying, 'What will we eat?' or 'What will we drink?' or 'What will we wear for clothing?' For the Gentiles eagerly seek all these things; for your heavenly Father knows that you need all these things. But seek first His kingdom and His righteousness, and all these things will be added to you. "So do not worry about tomorrow; for tomorrow will care for itself Each day has enough trouble of its own." (Matthew 6:19–21, 25–34)

## How Did We Get So Victim Focused?

God does not promise us a life on this earth without difficulties, but what He does promise is that His grace is sufficient to carry us through anything that this world may throw at us. All we must do is be faithful to follow His plan for our lives and to rely totally on Him. As Dr. Charles Stanley says, "Just obey God in everything, and leave the consequences of doing so completely in His hands. He will equip us and carry us through whatever we do as long as we are obeying what He tells us to do."

Only by taking our eyes off God's plan for us do we fall victim to the troubles of this world. That is what SATAN is trying to get every human to do because he knows that when we do, we lose our effectiveness as a witness for God. When we do that, we become vulnerable to SATAN'S deception that can make us victims. It is our choice, but God's will and His plan for our lives is the only choice in life that is guaranteed to provide us the maximum joy in this earthly life AND for us to store up treasures in Heaven that we will enjoy forever.

> *Our Father in Heaven, please forgive me if I fail to recognize that Your plan for my life is the best choice I could ever make for how I live my life while here on this Earth. I ask you for reveal your plan for my life in such a way that I cannot mistake knowing that it comes from you. I reject SATAN and his deception attempts to make me feel so victimized that I cannot see your plan for my life. I thank you that you love me enough to give me salvation and eternity in Heaven. AMEN*

*Day 2*

# America's Founding Fathers Were Victims
## *But with God's Help Escaped That Victim-Status and Became Conquerors*

> "You will possess their land; I will give it to you as an inheritance, a land flowing with milk and honey. I am the LORD your God."
>
> LEVITICUS 20:24

MANY OF THE ORIGINAL settlers of our great nation came here because they sought religious freedom. In the countries they came here from, they were unable to worship God as their consciences dictated, and frequently were discriminated against because of their religious beliefs. In those days, governments frequently declared the faith of their monarchs as the official state religion of the country they headed, and anyone not a member of that church faced discrimination and possible criminal punishment for not being a member of the official state church.

Those original settlers faced the perils of a four-month ocean voyage to America in small wooden boats where perhaps as many as a hundred-plus people were in crowded and unsanitary conditions. They faced treacherous Atlantic storms, dreadful cold, poor food, and many other hardships because of their determination to worship God according to their beliefs. Once here, they faced the difficulties of building shelters from the harsh winters, killing and growing enough food to feed and carry them through the winters. Of the original five-hundred settlers, only sixty survived the first winter.

For over one hundred years, as the nation grew, the settlers were victimized by the King of England where they had to deal with what they felt were unreasonable grievances imposed by the King. Here is the text of the Declaration of Independence where author Thomas Jefferson enumerates those grievances:

*"The history of the present King of Great Britain is a history of repeated injuries and usurpations, all having in direct object the establishment of an absolute Tyranny over these States. To prove this, let Facts be submitted to a candid world.*

- *He has refused his Assent to Laws, the most wholesome and necessary for the public good.*
- *He has forbidden his Governors to pass Laws of immediate and pressing importance, unless suspended in their operation till his Assent should be obtained; and when so suspended, he has utterly neglected to attend to them.*
- *He has refused to pass other Laws for the accommodation of large districts of people, unless those people would relinquish the right of Representation in the Legislature, a right inestimable to them and formidable to tyrants only.*
- *He has called together legislative bodies at places unusual, uncomfortable, and distant from the depository of their public Records, for the sole purpose of fatiguing them into compliance with his measures.*
- *He has dissolved Representative Houses repeatedly, for opposing with manly firmness his invasions on the rights of the people.*
- *He has refused for a long time, after such dissolutions, to cause others to be elected; whereby the Legislative powers, incapable of Annihilation, have returned to the People at large for their exercise; the State remaining in the meantime exposed to all the dangers of invasion from without, and convulsions within.*
- *He has endeavored to prevent the population of these States; for that purpose obstructing the Laws for Naturalization of Foreigners; refusing to pass others to encourage their migrations hither and raising the conditions of new Appropriations of Lands.*

## Don't Be a Victim: Choose Victory!

- *He has obstructed the Administration of Justice, by refusing his Assent to Laws for establishing Judiciary powers.*
- *He has made Judges dependent on his Will alone, for the tenure of their offices, and the amount and payment of their salaries.*
- *He has erected a multitude of New Offices and sent hither swarms of Officers to harass our people, and eat out their substance.*
- *He has kept among us, in times of peace, Standing Armies without the Consent of our legislatures.*
- *He has affected to render the Military independent of and superior to the Civil power.*
- *He has combined with others to subject us to a jurisdiction foreign to our constitution, and unacknowledged by our laws; giving his Assent to their Acts of pretended Legislation:*
- *For Quartering large bodies of armed troops among us:*
- *For protecting them, by a mock Trial, from punishment for any Murders which they should commit on the Inhabitants of these States:*
- *For cutting off our Trade with all parts of the world:*
- *For imposing Taxes on us without our Consent:*
- *For depriving us in many cases, of the benefits of Trial by Jury:*
- *For transporting us beyond Seas to be tried for pretended offences*
- *For abolishing the free System of English Laws in a neighboring Province, establishing therein an Arbitrary government, and enlarging its Boundaries so as to render it at once an example and fit instrument for introducing the same absolute rule into these Colonies:*
- *For taking away our Charters, abolishing our most valuable Laws, and altering fundamentally the Forms of our Governments:*
- *For suspending our own Legislatures and declaring themselves invested with power to legislate for us in all cases whatsoever.*
- *He has abdicated Government here, by declaring us out of his Protection and waging War against us.*
- *He has plundered our seas, ravaged our Coasts, burnt our towns, and destroyed the lives of our people.*

- *He is at this time transporting large Armies of foreign Mercenaries to compleat the works of death, desolation and tyranny, already begun with circumstances of Cruelty & perfidy scarcely paralleled in the most barbarous ages, and totally unworthy the Head of a civilized nation.*
- *He has constrained our fellow Citizens taken Captive on the high Seas to bear Arms against their Country, to become the executioners of their friends and Brethren, or to fall themselves by their Hands.*
- *He has excited domestic insurrections amongst us and has endeavored to bring on the inhabitants of our frontiers, the merciless Indian Savages, whose known rule of warfare, is an undistinguished destruction of all ages, sexes, and conditions.*

These grievances, along with the settlers' desire to live free to determine their own destinies and to worship God according to their own consciences, drove them to declare their independence from England, to fight a nearly seven year war against the best Navy and Army in the world at that time. The toll on the citizens of the then-colonies was huge, but they stood the test, and in the fall of 1781, General Cornwallis surrender his army at the battle of Charleston, South Carolina. On September 3, 1783, the Treaty of Paris was signed formally ending the conflict and confirming the establishment of America as a separate nation and no longer part of the British Empire.

How could a poorly organized group of independent states barely over one hundred years in existence defeat the strongest military country on the earth at the time? As William Novak, a Catholic scholar at the time said, "In all moments of imminent danger, as the first Act of the First Continental Congress, the founding generation turned to prayer"

The First Continental Congress took place on September 5, 1774. They opened that session with a time of Bible reading and prayer. As the leader of the session, Reverend Jacob Duche, an Anglican minister, read the entire 35th Psalm. As Eddie Hyatt writes in his article called "How Prayer Won the American Revolution," "... As the Psalm was read, a unique sense of God's presence filled the room and tears flowed from many eyes. John Adams (2nd President of the United States) wrote to his wife Abigail "Who can realize the emotions with which they turned imploringly to heaven for divine interposition and aid. It was enough to melt a heart of stone. I never saw a greater effect upon an audience. It seems as if heaven had ordained that Psalm to be read that day. I saw tears gush into the eyes of the old, grave pacific Quakers of Philadelphia. I must beg you to read that Psalm."

Story after story exists reporting the prayers of the founders for the victory during that Revolutionary war, and then when gathered together to adopt the Constitution of the United States in 1789, For an excellent article on the way prayer helped win the Revolutionary War, check this link out: *https://www.charismanews.com/opinion/58201-how-prayer-won-the-american-revolution*

Our founders believed that the freedoms we enjoy comes from God, not from man, and therefore are "inalienable," not subject to the governance of man, but only to the God who granted them. Through that Revolutionary War, America overcame its victimization by the King of England and gained its independence as a nation of free individuals who could worship God the way their consciences dictate.

The battle to overcome the feeling of being victimized should begin with the encouragement we receive from seeing how Christ overcame death on the cross through His Resurrection and the world of sin to die on the cross at Calvary as the final sacrifice to God for the forgiveness of sin and for the gift of eternal salvation through Christ Jesus. Anyone can receive these gifts from Christ simply by acknowledging and accepting His offer of salvation through belief in Him as God's son.

> *Father, I thank you for the privilege of being born an American. I thank you for the wisdom and courage of our founding fathers to seek your Divine guidance in virtually every step they took in winning our freedom from Great Britain and in establishing the best government system to manage the greatest nation you have ever put on this earth. Please forgive our sins as a nation. Never let us forget the sacrifice our founding fathers made, and their wisdom that they demonstrated during the establishment and formulation of our system of government. LORD, please draw America back to you as a nation that acknowledges Your divine Guidance in the birthing of America, and the courage to do whatever is necessary so our children and grandchildren can grow up in a nation where they are free to dream their dreams and work without the government interfering towards the achievement of their goals that you establish for their lives. AMEN*

*Day 3*

# Why I Believe God Is Real, Alive, Active in Our Lives and Loves Us All

"In the beginning was the Word, and the Word was with God, and the Word was God. He was in the beginning with God. All things were made through Him, and without Him was not anything made that was made. In Him was life and the life was the light of men. The light shines in the darkness, and the darkness has not overcome it"

JOHN 1:1 5 (ESV)

READING THIS SCRIPTURE, WE get a picture of something difficult to fathom. God has always existed. He created EVERYTHING! Man, the mountains, the galaxies, solar systems, stars, planets, moons, plants, animals, and even the air we breathe and the waters we drink. He created us humans! All this is told to us in the first book and chapter of the Bible, Genesis 1, by Moses, who is credited with writing the first five books of the Bible, called the Pentateuch (Genesis, Exodus, Leviticus, Numbers, and Deuteronomy).

Reading these books, one would logically ask "how would someone know what and how things happened thousands of years before his birth?" There were no printing presses, no typewriters, computers, printers, or even libraries before this, so how did this history get documented? The only answer comes from Moses himself. Throughout these books, Moses continually used terms like "the LORD said . . . ," "thus says the LORD," etc. In other words, God communicated directly with Moses, and through these discussions with God, Moses was given what to write.

The same happened repeatedly throughout the ages. God communicated with and inspired forty different individuals over a period of about fifteen-hundred years, living on three different continents, in three different languages to write about what He revealed to them, about their own interactions with God and Jesus, and about the lessons that God and Jesus taught them.

Most of the individuals that wrote the Bible never met the other authors, until the advent of Jesus and His apostles. There, in the New Testament, we have the eight different authors writing twenty-seven different books (Paul himself wrote 13). Every author in the New Testament encountered Jesus personally, either before or after His resurrection. They were taught by Him personally. Most witnessed His death and resurrection. Over five-hundred people personally encountered Jesus after His resurrection. Three of the Disciples witnessed Jesus' transformation and ascension into Heaven.

Voddy Baucham, a Bible Scholar and historian puts it like this: "*We have a reliable collection of historical documents written by eyewitnesses during the lifetimes of other eyewitnesses. They report supernatural events that took place in fulfillment of specific prophesies (in the Old Testament), and claim that their writings are Divine, rather than human in origin.*"

Depending on which Bible scholars one talks with, here are somewhere between three hundred and four hundred Old Testament prophesies which point to the coming of Jesus. Jesus fulfilled every one of them. The youngest of these prophesies in in the last book of the old Testament, Malachi 3:1–6:

> "*Behold, I send my messenger, and he will prepare the way before me. And the LORD whom you seek will suddenly come to his temple; and the messenger of the covenant in whom you delight, behold, he is coming, says the LORD of hosts. But who can endure the day of his coming, and who can stand when he appears? For he is like a refiner's fire and like fullers' soap. He will sit as a refiner and purifier of silver, and he will purify the sons of Levi and refine them like gold and silver, and they will bring offerings in righteousness to the LORD. Then the offering of Judah and Jerusalem will be pleasing to the LORD as in the days of old and as in former years.*
>
> "*Then I will draw near to you for judgment. I will be a swift witness against the sorcerers, against the adulterers, against those*

> who swear falsely, against those who oppress the hired worker in his wages, the widow and the fatherless, against those who thrust aside the sojourner, and do not fear me, says the LORD of hosts."

The book of Malachi was written over the period of 790–640 before the birth of Christ. The oldest was written in Genesis between 1450 BC and 1410 BC (before Christ) during the forty years that the Jews wandered in the desert. Scholars date it back as far as 1999 BC.

There is no other religion other than Christianity where there are so many authors, spread out over such a long period of time, from so many nations, who all claim that their writing are not their own, but were given to them and inspired by God Himself, and in which the Messiah (Savior) is prophesized. Likewise, this is the only book in the world where a Savior is promised, where His birth by a virgin and crucifixion on a cross are prophesized over seven hundred years before they occurred.

The Bible is the only book where every translation into different languages is derived from over six thousand original scrolls which have been recovered and translated, and where the translations are validated by the Rosetta Stone which was discovered in the 18th century (1799). That stone provided a tool which validated the translations from centuries before by saying the same thing in multiple different languages used in the ancient scrolls.

The claims of disbelievers range from all the writings being myths, written by men, translated improperly, and inaccurate in dates, has been disproved by tons of evidence found in over 28,000 archeological digs throughout the world. Virtually every assertion trying to justify the disbeliefs about its accuracy, time frames, misinterpretations, mistranslations, etc., have all been evidentially disproved or discredited.

And while all the evidence is reassuring to the believer and followers of Christ, yet there are still skeptics and those who just refuse to believe or even consider that they might be wrong. What are they missing? One simple fact: The real proof of the truth of the Bible comes through a simple, childlike act of faith. It occurs when one reaches that point that through the prompting and calling by God to accept His invitation to be forgiven of all their sins and receive a promise of life after physical death in Heaven and fellowshipping with God, by simply accepting Jesus as the Messiah, God's son, with childlike faith. Jesus was the ultimate and last sacrifice required by God for mankind's eternal salvation. Once that step of faith is taken, once one accepts that, asks Jesus to be their Savior and Messiah, the Holy spirit of God indwells every believer, and through that Holy Spirit, the assurance of our faith is given.

Paraphrasing Pastor Francis Chan, Before Jesus, God was this unapproachable, holy figure that had specific instructions for the priests that were allowed in the Temple at specific times, wearing specific clothes, and the animal sacrifices had to be made with specific animals in specific ways. Violations of these specific rules meant death.

God had given humans specific laws through the Ten Commandments. For centuries after they were given to Moses on Mt. Sinai, the Jewish religious leaders kept interpreting them, adding to them, and making them impossible to comply with for the ordinary man. Instead of the laws honoring God, those Jewish religious leaders manipulated the interpretations so that they honored and enriched themselves. Through the centuries, the people would fall away, God would allow them to be enslaved, then they would repent and cry out to God, and God would deliver them. Prophets kept telling the people that at some point, God was going to send a Messiah, a Savior, and the Jewish kingdom would be restored forever.

When Jesus arrived, He was not at all what the Jewish leaders were expecting. They were expecting a king like David, a warrior leader, righteous with God, who would militarily defeat all Israel's enemies. Instead, they got Jesus, the God man, who associated with the poor more than the rich, who preached repentance of sin, gave them instructions which did not do away with the Ten Commandments but instead took them another step. For example, "Thou Shalt not Kill" which had been always associated with physical murder. Instead Jesus said that if we hate somebody in our heart, that is equivalent to physical murder. When discussing "Thou Shalt Not Commit Adultery," Jesus said that looking at a woman with lust in our hearts is the equivalent in God's eyes to committing adultery.

Jesus' ministry was to change the way people thought; to turn their eyes away from the physical world and instead get them focusing on their spiritual body and soul. His purpose was to get humans to prioritize telling others about the eternal salvation that was theirs simply for the asking. He told people that God was a God of love. He broke all the ritualistic dogma that the Jewish leaders had imposed on the people, and made it childlike simple to be forgiven of sin, to be saved and guaranteed a life after death fellowshipping with God simply by accepting Jesus as God's son, and the promised Messiah from the old Testament.

*Why I Believe God Is Real, Alive, Active in Our Lives and Loves Us All*

When I think about the promises of God, the reason God created mankind, and all the references in scripture of how God loves us, it is difficult to feel like I am a victim of anything that cannot be overcome with God's promised love and help (Philippians 4:13). How can I feel victimized and defeated when I have a God that promises to never abandon me or leave me alone (Hebrews 13:5); that is with me constantly (Matthew 28:20), living as the Holy Spirit within me (1 Corinthians 3:16). How can I feel victimized and defeated when I have a God promises He will meet my every need (Philippians 4:9); that wants to bless me beyond anything I can imagine if I only trust (Luke 6:38 & Malachi 3:10)? Simple answer . . . I cannot! God has kept His promises to me in every instance where I have trusted Him and let Him lead my directions and life. I was a victim, but no longer! With God's help, I have overcome and have victory through Jesus!

This book is simply one man's way of trying to explain to others the wonderful feeling that exists between himself and God when the truth of salvation is revealed through Jesus. I will do my best to describe the relationship, but nothing I say or do can come close to experiencing it for oneself. I encourage everyone who reads this to pray about allowing Jesus to save you for eternity. I encourage everyone who reads this to believe that the alternative of eternity separated from God in Hell is a real choice, but hopefully one that will be avoided by accepting Christ as his or her Savior. I encourage everyone who reads this to realize that through Jesus, believers overcome evil, they overcome hell, they overcome victimization, and they become conquerors, lifetime victors over death and damnation, and destruction, and eternal winners in Heaven.

> *Heavenly Father, thank you for Jesus. Thank you for loving me enough to send me Your word and assurance that through Jesus, I can be assured of spending eternity in Heaven with you when I close my eyes in death here on earth. I pray that those reading this book will be reassured of their salvation if they have already accepted you, or if one has not yet done so, this book will give them the assurances needed to do so. AMEN*

## Day 4

# Who and/or What Is the Christian God?

Moses said to God, "Suppose I go to the Israelites and say to them, 'The God of your fathers has sent me to you,' and they ask me, 'What is his name?' Then what shall I tell them?" God said to Moses, "I am who I am." This is what you are to say to the Israelites: 'I am has sent me to you.'" God also said to Moses, "Say to the Israelites, 'The LORD the God of your fathers—the God of Abraham, the God of Isaac and the God of Jacob—has sent me to you.' This is my name forever, the name you shall call me from generation to generation."

EXODUS 3:13–15

I am the Alpha and the Omega, the First and the Last,
the Beginning and the End.

REVELATION 22:13(NIV)

GOD IS NOT A former human being. He is a spirit that has always been and will always be. He created everything, including man (Genesis 1:1–33). It is interesting to note that God used the term "us" when He talked about creation: *"And God said, let us make man in our image, after our likeness" Genesis 1:26*. God is a Trinity; the Father (God), the Son (Jesus), and the Holy Spirit. Jesus confirms this when He says that after He is gone, He will send a "helper," the Holy Spirit, to live within us, the third part of the Holy Trinity. It is easier to tell you who God is NOT. God is not a myth; God is

## Who and/or What Is the Christian God?

NOT an alien; God is NOT this evil judge just sitting around in Heaven waiting for us to mess us so he can send us to Hell. He is NOT the ultimate Santa Clause that we can pray to for wealth like Bill Gates, health like an Olympic gymnast, or a knight in shining army that will rescue us every time we get ourselves into trouble. But He is a God who is just; a God who hates sin, wants to bless us while here on this earth, and wants us to believe that His Son Jesus is the Messiah that was promised thousands of years before he came to become the ultimate sacrifice to God that would provide forgiveness of our sins and a guarantee of eternity in Heaven for all who would accept Jesus as their Savior.

Skeptics will try to convince people that there is no physical proof of God's existence. Yet when one reads in Genesis the description of Creation, and when we look at many of science's latest revelations about the age of the Universe, the historical and geological data being produced about the evolution of the earth, the evidence is overwhelmingly there validating the description of Creation in the Bible. One visit to the Creation Museum (https://creationmuseum.org) and the re-construction of Noah's Ark https://arkencounter.com/) and it is almost impossible for someone to at least not keep an open mind about the truth of the creation as described in the Bible.

In a recent poll, eighty-four percent of the world's population say they believe in a god, and fully one-third of the world say they are Christians. People all over the world, from the largest metropolitan areas to the remotest native tribes in the Amazon worship a supreme being. There is something inside a person that intuitively knows that there is something or someone, a supreme being or entity that created humans and all other living things. Add to this that there has been, and I believe never will be, any possible way that science will ever be able to prove that our world "evolved" somehow from a single cell entity into the variety of different species of animals and plants that exist on the planet today. That "missing link" has never been found, and frankly I believe it will never be found because it does not exit. The argument over creation is, in my opinion, one that has been raised by humans in search of a way to deny their reliance upon, their responsibility to, and/or their eventual judgment by an eternal God that created them and all other forms of matter in the universe. Some skeptics simply choose to deny that there really is an existence after death so they can delude themselves into believing that they can just go through life doing whatever they think is right because after they are dead, that is it . . . just oblivion. Other skeptics says that there is no hell; that a loving God would not condemn somebody that tries to live a "good life" to hell just because they do not believe the truth that Jesus Christ is God's only son and the Savior of the world is the only way to Heaven. The discussions of these beliefs have taken up untold numbers of volumes to articulate over the two thousand plus years since the advent of Christ and will continue to do the same until Christ's return. People are always looking for "proof" for their faith. Well, the Bible sums up the outcome of all these discussions and our choices. In the Paul's epistle of Hebrews, faith is described as *"Now faith is being sure of what we hope for and certain of what we do not see."* Hebrews 11:1 (NIV)

My personal faith has been an experience of growth. I accepted Christ as a young pre-teen child. I guess you could use the old term, I had "child-like" faith when I accepted Jesus. From there until now, however, that child-like faith has been confirmed to me in more ways that I can list. Almost daily now, God reveals his love for me, the truth of the Bible to me, and the reassurance of my faith to me. My faith has become a constant companion to me; something that is always just below the surface of my active conscience, and frequently its truth being spotlighted and brought to my attention during every day. I see things that non-Christians would call coincidence, but without the revelations shown me from God are totally inexplicable and would not make any sense absence the presence of a living, active God guiding my steps, protecting me from the attacks of Satan, and showing me the joys associated with being His servant. The proof to me came after stepping out in child-like faith, over the years through many ups and downs, fears, and victories, right and wrong choices. I would have it no other way.

The Christian religion is the only religion where the central person on earth of that religion did not stay dead once they died. Christ overcame the grave after being crucified, just as He had predicted to numerous crowds and individuals prior to His death. He appeared to over five-hundred different individuals after his death as documented in the Gospels written by his followers after His death

> *"For what I received I passed on to you as of first importance: that Christ died for our sins according to the Scriptures, that he was buried, that he was raised on the third day according to the Scriptures, and that he appeared to Cephas, and then to the Twelve. After that, he appeared to more than five hundred of the brothers and sisters*

> at the same time, most of whom are still living, though some have fallen asleep. Then he appeared to James, then to all the apostles, and last of all he appeared to me also, as to one abnormally born..."
> 1 Corinthians 15:3–9 (NIV)

Christ's existence has also been documented throughout the ages by various religions. Even the Jewish religion, which denied His divinity and had Him crucified, does not dispute His existence. Even the staunchest enemy of Christianity, the Islamic radical extremists acknowledge His existence and classify Him as a great prophet and teacher.

Christ proclaimed Himself as the promised Messiah, as the Son of God, and as part of the Trinity when He said the Father and He are the same, and when He said that if one has seen Him, one has seen the Father (*"I and the Father are One"* John 10:30 (NIV)); *("I tell you the truth . . . before Abraham was born, I am"*! John 8:58 (NIV). NOTICE: *Jesus uses the same words to describe Himself here as God the Father did to describe Himself to Moses some 1400+ years before the birth of Christ).* As a Christian, I believe all of that. I believed it at first because I was raised in the Methodist Church, and at some point, I asked Christ to be my personal Savior because that is what the preacher said I had to do to go to Heaven. Later I believed it because I experienced God very personally while in Vietnam. I prayed diligently for some truth, so I could know that my faith was going to get me into Heaven. I heard a voice that seemed loud as though spoken out loud in my barracks room while sleeping. It woke me up, but when I looked around, all my three roommates were sound asleep. The voice confirmed my faith and confirmed to me the truth of the Bible. I will never forget what I heard that night "Stick with what you know to be the truth!." I went to some friends and woke them up and asked them what they thought the words might mean. These were two people of another religion that were trying to convince me to join that religion. They proclaimed Christ as the son of God, but also claimed that there was another prophet of God that had been given a translation of ancient texts that came and re-established the original Christian church on earth. After initially saying that they really did not know what to think of it, one offered the explanation that maybe Satan was trying to deceive me somehow. Without thinking, I said "Why would Satan tell me to stick with the Holy Bible?" Neither had an answer. That thought had never entered my mind until they said what they did. I will go to my grave believing that God spoke to me and told me that the Holy Bible was, indeed, His Holy Scripture, was His truth given to man as

## Don't Be a Victim: Choose Victory!

a guide for us to live and could be trusted. I have never doubted it since. I cannot understand some of the conflicts from old to new testaments, but I presume they have something to do with Christ establishing a "New Covenant" while He was on the earth. As I say, I cannot understand everything in the Bible, but I do not question the truth of what it says. Does the fact that I cannot understand everything in the Bible bother me? Not really. The Scriptures tell us that we will not understand everything. *"For my thoughts are not your thoughts, neither are your ways my ways," declares the LORD. "As the heavens are higher than the earth, so are my ways higher than your ways and my thoughts than your thoughts."* (Isaiah 55:8-9). Think about this ... do we really want a God that thinks like we think? I know I do not! I am wise enough to know that my thoughts are evil at times. I want a God that is better than I am; that offers me relief from my sinful thoughts and wicked ways. I want a God worthy of my worship and reverence and praise; not one that is as weak and sinful as me.

In today's "show me" society, where something is not believable to much of the world unless they can prove it scientifically, I believe that God is still revealing Himself in ways that, in my mind, are inexplicable except that God is real and loves us enough to show himself so that everyone can believe.

For example, take the case of a young three-year-old boy named Colton Burpo. Colton almost died on an operating table and went to Heaven and met Jesus, saw his grandfather, sat on Jesus' lap, and met a sister that died while still in Mom's womb before Colton was born. Colton's grandfather died many years before he was born. When Colton's father showed him a picture of his grandfather as an old man, Colton did not recognize him. But when asked to pick out a younger grandad from among a bunch of pictures of younger men, Colton immediately picked out his grandad. The sister that died in womb was never given a name by the Mom and Dad. When Colton said he met her in Heaven and asked her name, she said she did not have one because her Mom and Dad never gave her one.

But the clincher circumstance to me was when the Dad kept asking Colton what Jesus looked like. He showed him every picture depicting Jesus that he could find, but none of them were what Colton said He looked like. Now, enter a young Russian girl living in Chicago, hundreds of miles away from Colton, named Akiane Kramarik. Akiane also had visions where God showed her Heaven and Jesus, and God encouraged her to draw and paint her visions. One of them entitled Prince of Peace was an oversize canvas painting of Jesus as she said he looked when she meant him during one of her visions in Heaven.

Colton's dad never found a picture that Colton said was Jesus, However, one day, when Akiane was on TV, Colton's Dad happened to see the interview. During that interview, when they were showing the huge picture she painted of Jesus, Colton came in from playing outside, walked by the TV, saw the picture, and very plainly and calmly said "that's him," that the picture was the Jesus whose lap he sat on when he visited Heaven. Colton was then four or five years old and had never met nor heard of Akiane before. Colton's family did not know of her. Yet she said she saw Jesus in her visions and painted him, then Colton sits on his lap in Heaven, then when he stumbled into the house and in front of the TV when Akiane's painting is on TV and tells his Dad that the picture was the same Jesus he saw in Heaven. Coincidence? Not in my humble opinion.

I will acknowledge that there are many who would look at these occurrences and list many possible explanations for "coincidences" like this. Theologically, we must be warned that relying on incidents as depicted above as "proof" of God's existence or of justification for believing in Christ might not be the best of reasons for doing so, because then when some alternative explanation from the secular world is put forth, it might shake the foundations of our faith. The reason for believing in Christ as one's Savior should be the revelation through the Scriptures and prayer that Christ is calling to us to follow Him because the Holy Scriptures are true, and that through the acceptance of the truth of Scriptures with child-like faith we will have our sins forgiven, and will spend eternity in Heaven with God once we close our eyes in death.

As I mentioned earlier, once that acceptance of Jesus as our Savior has taken place, it is my belief that we as believers can then see the "proofs" of the truth of the Scriptures that God reveals to us and the world as encouragements for believers and seekers.

Every real Christian has encountered something in their life where Jesus becomes very real to them. It has happened to virtually everyone I have talked with that I know is a real Christian. God is good like that.

Why is this important to those of us who have times when we feel like the whole world is out to get us; like we are victims of a cruel and vicious fate out to make our lives miserable? Because all of us are looking for something or someone that we can always count on to be on our side. We want something that gives us hope, someone to love and that loves us

## Don't Be a Victim: Choose Victory!

unconditionally and that we can have absolute faith in to never leave us alone to face the evils of this earth. Jesus has proven to me over and over that He is that someone who is always there, that someone who intercedes for me when I fail to live up to God's expectations. He is that someone who, through His sacrifice on the cross of Calvary, provides me a guaranteed entry into Heaven and who is a constant companion that I carry in my spirit who is the Holy Spirit of Jesus, who never leaves me. Through Christ, I no longer must feel like a victim. I am an overcomer, someone that has, with and through my Savior Jesus Christ, overcome all efforts to make me feel victimized, hopeless, and frustrated. Through Christ, I feel redeemed. I feel like though the evil on earth may attack me and knock me down at times, with Christ's help, I can get up, and with Christ's help, I can overcome whatever is attacking me, trying to destroy me and trying to steal my joy of life. Through Christ, I will be victorious because I know that this life is only the beginning, and that Satan has been defeated by Christ and that nothing Satan can do will destroy me as if I cling to the promises that Christ has given me of never abandoning and never leaving me while I am on this earth. I am NOT a victim; I am a winner and a survivor.

> *Father, I thank you for revealing yourself to the world and coming to die in the form of your only begotten son, Jesus Christ, to take on the burden of the sins of all mankind forever. I cannot conceive of that kind of love, but I am eternally grateful for it. Thank you for being that loving of a God that you opened salvation to the whole world for any individual that would accept Jesus Christ as their Messiah and your son. I proclaim that belief now for the world to see, grateful for the love of a God so loving and kind to save a wretch like me. AMEN*

# Day 5

## You Are Not Alone—Ever

Nevertheless, I am continually with you; you hold my right hand.
PSALM 73:23 (ESV)

Even though I walk through the valley of the shadow of death, I will fear no evil, for you are with me; your rod and your staff, they comfort me.
PSALM 23:4 (ESV)

Do you not know that you are God's temple and that God's Spirit lives in you? If someone destroys God's temple, God will destroy him. For God's temple is holy, which is what you are.
1 CORINTHIANS 3:16-17

What? know ye not that your body is the temple of the Holy Ghost which is in you, which ye have of God, and ye are not your own?
1 CORINTHIANS 6:19

ONE OF THE WORST feelings I deal with at times is feeling totally alone with my problems because there are just some things that I cannot share. I have no-one that I feel like I can talk to because they just cannot "understand."

## Don't Be a Victim: Choose Victory!

The verses above are a great comfort to me in those times. They reassure me that I am NEVER alone because God is right there with me. Scriptures continually remind me that though both of my birth parents are dead, because of the sacrifice of Jesus Christ, God's only son, who died taking on the burden of my and every other human's sins, I have a heavenly Father that is always with me. The very last words that Jesus spoke to His disciples as he ascended into Heaven reconfirms to us that we are never alone: *"Go therefore and make disciples of all the nations, baptizing them in the name of the Father and the Son and the Holy Spirit, teaching them to observe all that I commanded you; and lo, I am with you always, even to the end of the age."* Matthew 28:19–20

I am in awe of God! I continually wonder why the creator of the universe, a being that is totally omnipresent (is everywhere at once), omniscient (knows all), and omnipotent (all powerful), who needs nothing, would even allow me to exist as many times as I fail Him daily. But even as I write this, I know the answer, and it has nothing to do with me. It is because of one simple childlike act that I committed decades ago, and that is because I responded to that feeling inside of me telling me that I needed to accept His Son Jesus Christ as my Savior. In that moment, God forgave me of all my sins to that point and for the rest of my life. Each time I pray and confess my sins to Jesus, God washes me clean and declares me "righteous," someone worthy of being allowed to pray to, fellowship with, and be loved by a holy, righteous God. What a humbling gift! Jesus' sacrifice on the cross of Calvary washes away my sins forever with His blood. Now God does not see me as a sinner; instead, He sees me as one of His children through the vail of the blood of Jesus, I am washed clean and am presentable and acceptable to my Creator.

I am struck almost dumbfounded by that. What an amazing God! A God that loves me and wants to fellowship with me. Even though there are six billion plus people on this planet, the Creator of every one of us wants to fellowship with me! That realization humbles me to the point of tears, excites me to the point of shouting "THANK YOU JESUS" to the world at the top of my lungs!

It also inspires me to want to let everybody know what a wonderful God we have. Not only does God love us, but He wants to bless us!

> *"Ask, and it will be given to you; seek, and you will find; knock, and it will be opened to you. For everyone who asks receives, and he who seeks finds, and to him who knocks it will be opened. Or what man*

> is there among you who, when his son asks for a loaf, will give him a stone? Or if he asks for a fish, he will not give him a snake, will he? If you then, being evil, know how to give good gifts to your children, how much more will your Father who is in heaven give what is good to those who ask Him! In everything, therefore, treat people the same way you want them to treat you, for this is the Law and the Prophets." Matthew 7:7-12.

In the Scripture verses above, Jesus tells believers that if we ask for something that God knows would be good for us, we will receive it! God knows each one of His children intimately, and as a loving Father who only wants what is best for us *with relation to our spiritual and physical health and wellbeing*. If what we request meets that criteria, we can count on God to deliver it. As the Scripture above states, God will not necessarily give us something that will harm our spiritual or physical wellbeing. But the Scripture demonstrates that God is a very generous, loving Father and wants to provide for both our needs as a human, but more importantly our needs as an eternal spiritual being in Heaven once our earth lives are done.

In the next chapter, I will try to present some both spiritual proof and some logical proof both for the existence of God, for the resurrection, and some question and answers as to why one should NOT be an atheist, Buddhist, Muslim, or any other religion but Christian. Though circumstances may make us feel like a victim, the Holy Spirit living within we Christians reminds us that we are victors over death, victors over our sinful nature, and that no matter what the world does to us as humans, eventually when we go to Heaven, we are victors over all that wished to make us victims.

> Heavenly Father, thank You for Your promise that we will never be alone once we accept Your SON Jesus Christ as our Savior. Thank you for Your gift of an indwelling of Your Holy Spirit to guide us, to intercede with You for us when we need guidance, when we do not know the words that we need to pray to You that express our heart. Thank You for the realization that we will are never alone; that when we feel the whole world makes us feel like victims and that everyone has abandoned us, that no-one understands us, and that we have no-where to turn, the reality is that You are always there, waiting for us to accept Your promise, *"Come to me, all who labor and are heavy laden, and I will give you rest. Take my yoke upon you, and learn from me, for I am gentle and lowly in heart, and you will find rest for your souls. For my yoke is easy, and my burden is light."* AMEN Matthew 11:28-30 (ESV)

*Day 6*

## Are Heaven and Hell Real Places?

Then I saw a new heaven and a new earth, for the first heaven and the first earth had passed away, and the sea was no more. And I saw the holy city, new Jerusalem, coming down out of heaven from God, prepared as a bride adorned for her husband. And I heard a loud voice from the throne saying, "Behold, the dwelling place of God is with man. He will dwell with them, and they will be his people, and God himself will be with them as their God. He will wipe away every tear from their eyes, and death shall be no more, neither shall there be mourning, nor crying, nor pain anymore, for the former things have passed away." And he who was seated on the throne said, "Behold, I am making all things new." Also he said, "Write this down, for these words are trustworthy and true." And he said to me, "It is done! I am the Alpha and the Omega, the beginning, and the end. To the thirsty I will give from the spring of the water of life without payment. The one who conquers will have this heritage, and I will be his God and he will be my son. But as for the cowardly, the faithless, the detestable, as for murderers, the sexually immoral, sorcerers, idolaters, and all liars, their portion will be in the lake that burns with fire and sulfur, which is the second death."

REVELATION 21:1–8

IF YOU ARE ASKING yourself "what does the question of whether Heaven or hell are real places have to do with feeling victimized and the need to get over those feelings?," let me answer it as clearly as possible; it will make it clear that there is a way out of that feeling because one can feel confident that, as a Christian, God has provided us something far better than what we as victims are going through as a non-believer or a person who feels victimized and has no way out, so-to-speak.

The Bible is quite clear on whether Heaven and Hell are real or not. The referenced Scripture states it emphatically. The entire chapter goes on to describe the New Heaven which appears after the tribulation and Christ's return. It is a beautiful place physically, but what most people are looking forward to is the description in verse four: *"He will wipe away every tear from their eyes, and death shall be no more, neither shall there be mourning, nor crying, nor pain anymore, for the former things have passed away."*

Skeptics abound always saying that they cannot believe in something that they cannot see, or that the Bible is just a bunch of stories written by a bunch of old men that lived thousands of years ago, based on superstitions. Yet, according to several recent surveys, about eighty-five percent of the world believe in a "god" (https://www.answers.com/Q/What_percent_of_the_population_believe_in_God), and from fifty-one to fifty-three percent of the world's population believe in the Judeo-Christian God of the Bible (https://www.christianpost.com/news/global-poll-most-believe-in-god-afterlife.html).

Whether or not one chooses to believe in a god, or Jesus Christ, or whatever, most believe there is something after death. One can look all over the world and find instances where people died and were later resuscitated who experienced an after-death experience of some kind. The empirical evidence they present is undeniable to most. Those who refuse to believe these cases usually look for an excuse because they just do not want to believe. Others quote supposedly scientific studies that supposedly prove these were simply some type of neuro-stimulation bringing forth visions of some kind, sort of like dreams. But some cases are unexplainable unless there really is a Heaven; like Colton Burpo's description of what he saw in Heaven as a three year old, and Akiane Kramarik, who also visited Jesus in Heaven and painted a huge portrait of Jesus as she saw Him

These children lived hundreds of miles apart and had never met. Yet, when Colton walked in on his dad when he was watching a talk show where Akiane's portrait of Jesus was on the screen, Colton said the picture was Jesus as he saw Him in Heaven (Colton's Dad had shown him every picture he had seen of Jesus, but none were what Colton said he saw in Heaven before he saw Akiane's portrait on TV).

Colton and Akiane's stories are only two of thousands of persons who have documented cases of going to Heaven while clinically dead, then being resuscitated to tell their stories. In virtually all these instances, the person experienced something that was beautiful, where they did not want to leave, and where they felt peace and joy and happiness. Often, people recalled meeting loved ones that has passed, and the joy they felt was overwhelming. Many said they could not wait to get back and share what they had experienced because God told them that was what they were to do. Virtually all said that their lives were changed for the better.

Believing in Jesus gives one hope. Hope gives us something to look forward to, both in this life and after we die. The following Scriptures assure us that Christ is a way to have a more abundant life and will provide for all our needs. *John 10:10 "The thief comes only to steal and kill and destroy; I came that they may have life, and have it abundantly. Matthew 6:33 "But seek first His kingdom and His righteousness, and all these things will be added to you." Psalm 16:11 "You will make known to me the path of life; In Your presence is fullness of joy; In Your right hand there are pleasures forever."*

To summarize, the Bible described Heaven and hell. It tells us what it takes to go to Heaven once we die and warns of the horrible $2^{nd}$ death in the lake of fire and sulfur where those are tormented forever that refuse to accept Jesus as their Savior. But the promises of joy, peace, and life more abundant through accepting Christ give us hope, which help us escape the victim status in our minds. I accept these Scriptures on faith, however, and not just because of the evidence pointing to their being truthful. I accepted them decades ago before I knew about any "evidence," and through the years, Jesus has confirmed the truth of the Bible to me in ways that I describe as irrefutable. But that is just me. It is my prayer that all will accept Jesus; I cannot stand the thought of anyone having to spend eternity in hell when Jesus provides all the gift of salvation through faith in Him. The knowledge that there are those who will refuse His offer, however, both saddens and frustrated me greatly.

> *Dear Father in Heaven, thank you for the descriptions of Heaven and Hell in Your Word. I pray that everyone will accept the free offer of salvation through accepting Jesus Christ as Your Son and the Messiah. Thank you for the reassurance and affirmation of the Bible that you have given me over the years. I pray the scales be removed off*

*Are Heaven and Hell Real Places?*

*the eyes of the non-believer or those with doubts so they can receive Jesus' wonderful gift of Salvation and learn the pure joy that comes with having Jesus as our Savior.*

*Day 7*

# Dealing with Survivor's Guilt

> For you formed my inward parts; you knitted me together in my mother's womb. I praise you, for I am fearfully and wonderfully made. Wonderful are your works; my soul knows it very well. <sup>15</sup>My frame was not hidden from you, when I was being made in secret, intricately woven in the depths of the earth. <sup>16</sup>Your eyes saw my unformed substance; in your book were written, every one of them, the days that were formed for me, when as yet there was none of them.
>
> PSALM 139:13–16

WHEN I CAME HOME from Vietnam, I came home without a scratch. In 117 combat missions, my airplane never took damage from enemy fire. I know now that it was only the protective hand of God that allowed me to come home unscathed, but at the time I did not understand that. While I was in Southeast Asia, several of my friends were shot down and taken prisoner. The day I left to go to Vietnam, my pilot that I went through F4 training with, Captain Jeffrey L. Harris, was killed. While I was in Vietnam, a downstairs neighbor from Navigator school, Captain Sammy O'Donnell was killed. Every day I was there, American and South Vietnamese soldiers died in combat. On one mission my pilot and I were credited with over 240 enemy killed, a statistic I will never forget that bothers me more the longer I live.

Death happens in war, and frequently those deaths are the result of a freak accident or occurrence where the odds of being killed were so high

## Dealing with Survivor's Guilt

they are almost incalculable. Many missions I went on the odds of us losing an airplane were so high that on one particularly scary one, I had convinced myself the night before that I would die that day, and had made peace with God over that, but I and my pilot and our airplane survived without a scratch. Yet, on a mission where the odds of the airplane getting hit are almost incalculably low, one bullet hits the airplane and kills my old downstairs neighbor, Sammy. I have heard similar stories from my Army friends where two guys are fighting side by side, mere inches separating them, and one gets killed and one never receives a scratch. Bad luck, bad karma? No, not according to God's word. It simply was their time to go.

I cannot speak for others, but I asked myself why me, LORD? Why did Jeff or Major Whitt, or Andy, or Sammy die and not me? I have talked with many veterans from the Vietnam conflict, Desert Storm, and the current war in the Middle East where they lost friends and they ask themselves the same question. The truth is, we will never know for sure until we get to Heaven, but there is one comforting Scripture shown above that tells us why. Simply put, it was their time to die, not ours.

It was after I came back from Vietnam that this Scripture was shown and explained to me. I cannot remember how I found this Scripture; I just remember the impact on me when I read it and came to understand what it was telling me. I was always told that God has a plan for each of us; that we have the free will to follow that plan, or we have the free will to go it our own way. But either way, as that Scripture above says, God has written in His book all the days of our lives that we are supposed to live.

God sees life from end to end all at once. The way it was explained to me was that our life is like a big scroll rolled out all the way from beginning to end, and God can see it in its entirety all at once. And even though God gives us free will to do what we want with our lives, those of us who He has predestined to be His people who will live in Heaven with Him eternally, He knows the decisions we will make. Yes, there are cases when we can defy what was in the book by taking our own lives, but that is another discussion. Suffice it to say those that God has predestined to be his children and to accept Christ, He has our lives all mapped out for us and barring our deciding to defy His will for our lives and who will take our own lives, we will live the length of life that God has written in His book.

There are many questions about "predestination." Many will ask does this mean that God has picked and chosen before our births which of us will accept Christ and which will not? Does that sound like the loving God

## Don't Be a Victim: Choose Victory!

who says in Acts 2:21 that all who call on the name of the LORD (Jesus) will be saved? That term "all" says that to me that anyone who calls on the name of Jesus as the Christ to save them will be saved. And if only the predestined are to be saved, then why did Jesus while ascending to Heaven the final time tell his Disciples: *"Therefore go and make disciples of all nations, baptizing them in the name of the Father and of the Son and of the Holy Spirit, and teaching them to obey everything I have commanded you. And surely I am with you always, to the very end of the age."* Matthew 28:19–20? That seems clear that Jesus is telling His disciples to go to the rest of the world and tell His story and save as many people as they can.

Also, Peter says this in 2 Peter 3:9 "The LORD is not slow in keeping his promise, as some understand slowness. Instead He is patient with you, not wanting anyone to perish, but everyone to come to repentance" (NIV). Dr. Charles Stanley in his sermon *"The Foreknowledge of God-Part 2"* as heard on his website http://www.intouch.org (listen here: https://www.intouch.org/listen/featured/the-foreknowledge-of-god-part-2) explains that salvation itself it not predestined and is open to all who choose it. But since God is omniscient (knows all for all time), He knows who will be making the decisions to accept Jesus ahead of time, and has therefore prepared a plan for our lives which would provide us the most joy, peace, contentment, and preparation for our lives in Heaven with Him.

This still leaves a lot of questions unanswered; questions like "what if someone changes their mind that God did not expect to do so and decides to accept Jesus as their Savior? If God really is omniscient, that cannot happen, because God already knows who we are and what we will do before we are born. The Bible also says that our ways are not God's ways and that we cannot understand them all. That will have to be enough for us until we get to Heaven where the answers will not be needed, since we will be in our Heavenly bodies in eternal fellowship with God and His Son Jesus Christ.

To understand this truth is to then understand why we are alive, and our brothers and sisters killed in war are not. To understand this truth was, for me, a pivotal moment in my overcoming my survivor's guilt. There is still danger once we realize this, however. In my case, it was the recurring "if only" thoughts that kept returning. What if I had reported an incident where one of my friends who died over there had committed a serious and potentially fatal error during one of our training missions that could have killed us both had I not taken control of the airplane. Maybe he would not have been flying that day that he was killed. What if I had been there

## Dealing with Survivor's Guilt

flying with Jeff when he was killed? I knew Jeff's weaknesses and strengths probably better than he did, and maybe I could have prevented his death by watching his performance more closely than did his back seater that died with him. What if... What if...?

These types of questions filled me with anger; anger at myself for not doing what I knew I should have done because I was asked not to report an incident. Anger at not being there for Jeff. Anger for doing my job to preserve my airplane instead of risking it by staying on station so we could drop our bombs instead of leaving the scene when we were already below the minimum fuel requirements that our higher headquarters had established to reach the closest base without endangering the airplane and us. (By the way, when we finally touched down at Ben Hoi airport in Saigon, we had barely enough fuel remaining to allow us to taxi the aircraft to the parking ramp for re-arming and refueling. Had we stayed in our holding pattern even another minute, we would have run out of fuel before landing!)

My questions are different from every other soldier that fights survivor guilt. But the symptoms are the same. We get depressed, we wonder what we could have or should have done differently, if anything, which might have kept our friends alive. But when we stop and pray about it, and talk to others about our guilt, we find that we are not alone, and when forced to think rationally, we realize that nothing we could have done differently would have saved our friends, because of one reality; it was their time to go.

Accepting reality for what it is instead of what we want reality to be is a very freeing moment. Realizing that there was nothing we, or really nothing that anyone could have done to change that reality sets us free from the guilt we carry because they died, and we did not. In my case, it also made me incredibly grateful to God for the fact that I was alive, and it refocused my goals away from living for myself and has driven me towards finding a way to help others. Hopefully, I am helping people get past survivor's guilt. Hopefully, I am helping people get a totally different view towards who God is, how He loves us, and how we can gain a real purpose, and real peace by allowing God to take control of our lives and be used by Him to bring others to accept the gift of salvation through Jesus Christ and the eternal life in Heaven fellowshipping with Jesus that salvation provides.

Life is a precious gift, but in the view of eternity, our lives here on earth are but a whisper, a fleeting breath that comes and goes and passes into forever. We all will die. It is my prayer, however, that no-one be lost because of the deception from SATAN's lies. When one realizes the beauty that life holds when lived under the leadership of Christ, in my case, it has spawned an ever growing desire to spend more and more time fellowshipping with Jesus, to know Him better, and to serve Him better, and to not lose a single soul to SATAN's lies and eternity separated from God.

> *Heavenly Father, thank you for your Scriptures that teach us how deeply you love us, how deeply you desire to fellowship with us, how deeply You desire to bless us beyond our wildest dreams. Thank you for the lessons which can free us from the guilt we carry for surviving when so many of our friends were killed in the wars our nation has fought. Help us to always remember that through the sacrifice of Your only Son, Jesus Christ, we are freed from the guilt we carry, whether deserved or undeserved, and are washed as clean as snow so that we can fellowship with you for eternity. AMEN*

*Day 8*

# God Has a Plan for Our Lives
*The Path to a Joyful and Peaceful Existence*

"You make known to me the path of life; in your presence there is fullness of joy; at your right hand are pleasures forevermore."
PSALM 16:11, (ESV)

"Be joyful always; pray continually; give thanks in all circumstances, for this is God's will for you in Christ Jesus."
1 THESSALONIANS 5:16–18, (NIV)

"Rejoice in hope, be patient in tribulation, be constant in prayer."
ROMANS 12:12, (ESV)

"Never Stop Praying."
1 THESSALONIANS 5:17, (NLT)

"Rejoice in the LORD always; again I will say, Rejoice."
PHILIPPIANS 4:4, (ESV)

# Don't Be a Victim: Choose Victory!

"Don't act thoughtlessly, but understand what the LORD wants you to do.
EPHESIANS 5:17 (NLT)

PART OF FEELING LIKE a victim, at least for me, was that I never felt totally at peace, and I could never understand why. I was very insecure emotionally because of the turmoil in my life. I was the guy that looked at the glass and saw it half-empty, instead of half-full. I worried about my job, because subconsciously, I did not want to be doing what I was doing; I always wanted to fly fighters, and after I achieved that, I had to give up that career in order to try and salvage my marriage. I always knew I was cut out to be "different" than others, but I greatly misjudged what made me feel that way. Because of my experience in the Air Force, I had confidence in my own abilities to do any job that I was given, but I got no satisfaction from doing it because it really was not what I was cut out to do!

I also felt guilty because I was in a marriage that was not good. We went through the motions; we went to church, took our daughter to ballet and dance lessons, I taught Sunday School, was a church treasurer, and provided what I thought was very well for my family. But I could never fill that big hole in my spirit, because I really had no idea what was missing. I kept trying to find something in my work or in my marriage that might give me a feeling of peace, of security, and of satisfaction with the life I was living, but nothing ever did.

I knew I was a Christian, I knew God loved me, I knew that Jesus Christ had died so that I could have all my sins forgiven and go to Heaven when I died; there was no doubt in my mind of that. However, looking back, I now understand why that feeling continually eluded me. I was trying all on my own to find happiness, trying to make happen what I thought the plan for my life was. I had always wanted to fly fighter aircraft for my career. I had achieved that partially, becoming a back seater in the best aircraft in the world at that time, the F4 Phantom II fighter bomber, and had I stayed in the Air Force, could have applied to upgrade to the front seat by going through pilot training. Being a Vietnam Veteran and still having perfect eyesight, I was assured that I would have been accepted. But I had to pass on that opportunity to try and save my first marriage. The resentment for having to give up my dream had poisoned me for anything else I did as

## God Has a Plan for Our Lives

an employee. I kept thinking I could still make my own plans that would eventually lead me to satisfaction, joy, and peace.

It took many years of searching and unconsciously fighting God's plan for my life before I came to realize that I just could not do it on my own. It was not until after I literally gave up in anger and told God that I was tired of fighting Him and that from now on, if anything was to happen with me career wise, He would have to make it happen. I had been trying desperately for five years to make something happen, and within two weeks of my turning everything over to him, He showed me His grace and I went to the best job and location I had experienced in my civilian work.

Since that time, I have let God make ALMOST every decision that I thought was important in my life. I have relapsed into my old do-it-yourself mode a few times, and that always ended up as a mistake. Now, I am committed to turning everything over to God. Every decision! But how do we understand and learn what God's plan for our life is; how can we feel confident we are doing what God wants us to do with our lives?

Dr. Charles Stanley's sermon on his "In Touch Ministries" website (www.intouch.org) is entitled "He Will Show You His Will." In that sermon, he gives a logical and scripturally based answer to the question of how we can know what God's will is for our lives.

First, Dr. Stanley says that we must Trust God. We are not going to be willing to put our life into the hands of someone that we cannot trust. So that begs the question "is God Trustworthy?" To answer that, we can both use logic and then back that up with Scripture.

God is the creator of all. He created the sun, the moon, the stars, all the planets, and every living thing *(Genesis, chapters 1–3)*. He is omnipotent (all powerful), omniscient (all knowing), and omnipresent (present everywhere). Therefore, He cannot lie (think about it; every word God issues is truth because as the Creator, He has no superior power; He IS the ultimate power, so what He says has to be true, and what He does Has to be the right thing to do! Scripture teaches us that God loves us, that he created us to fellowship with Him, and that he has a plan for us, a plan to prosper us and not to harm us, so that we will pray to Him and worship him (*For I know the plans I have for you," says the LORD. "They are plans for good and not for disaster, to give you a future and a hope. In those days when you pray, I will listen. If you look for me wholeheartedly, you will find me. I will be found by you," says the LORD. "Jeremiah 29:11–14).*

## Don't Be a Victim: Choose Victory!

He is our Heavenly Father who loves us and wants to give us the best life possible here on this earth to prepare us for our heavenly home. If we have any sense, we should realize that God is the only person/entity/spirit that we can always trust completely and without doubt.

Second, we must learn to wait on God's timing in our lives. Humans by their very nature are impatient creatures. When we know we have something to do, especially something that we know is good for us, we want to do it as fast as possible. Sometimes, however, that is not God's timing. Even when we discern what God's will for us is, we must also then wait for God to tell us when we are to begin: *Wait patiently for the LORD. Be brave and courageous. Yes, wait patiently for the LORD. Psalm 27:14.*

This is probably the most difficult challenge in following God's will for our lives as revealed to us. But every day during our devotion time, we need to practice sitting quietly in prayer and meditation listening for God's input into our lives. He is faithful in doing so when our motives are pure as we seek to understand what His will for us is.

> *Dear Heavenly Father, thank you for Jesus, our Messiah, who provides for us forgiveness of our sins. LORD, we struggle daily in our efforts to live a life that follows Your plan for us. Help us each day to seek your plan for our lives; to listen quietly during our quiet time with you for your guidance. Give us the wisdom to discern what is your will, and the courage to follow it. AMEN*

*Day 9*

# Dealing with Being Prideful

"There are six things the LORD hates, seven that are detestable to him: haughty eyes, a lying tongue, hands that shed innocent blood, a heart that devises wicked schemes, feet that are quick to rush into evil, false witness who pours out lies and a person who stirs up conflict in the community.

PROVERBS 6:16-19 (NIV)

"*It's Not about You*"! These are the first words of *The Purpose Driven Life*, by Pastor Rick Warren of Saddleback Church in California. Pastor Rick is addressing the issue of pride. Why would the pastor of a church with an average attendance of 22,000 begin a book with this line? I can think of several possible explanations, but the one that first comes to mind is the statement in the Scripture quoted above. The verse quoted above states that there are six things God HATES in a person's behavior: Of the six things that God hates, the very first thing is "haughty eyes." Merriam Webster defines "Haughty" like this: "blatantly and disdainfully proud: having or showing an attitude of superiority and contempt for people or things perceived to be inferior ." Simply stated God hates the behavior of people that are self-absorbed, who think only of themselves in every situation, and who see themselves as better than everybody else.

If I am really going to trust God, then I need to stop trusting myself; I need to deal with my pride issue. God warns us about the state of being full of pride. *"Pride goes before destruction, a haughty spirit before a fall. Proverbs 16:18.* God warns humans that being arrogant, prideful, or haughty is an awfully bad character trait; avoid it all costs!

This is contradictory to what the world is teaching everyone today. Watch TV or go to the movies, see them promote self-gratification, self-accomplishment, and an attitude that "it is all about me!" as what should be sought. People are measured to be successful by our bosses, our friends, and by society in general on what we accomplish.

On the other hand, God has an entirely different measurement on what He expects from people. He expects us to trust Him instead of serving ourselves, we are to serve others. As a Christian, God's simple measure is this: "What have you done to bring others to a saving faith in My son Jesus Christ?" He wants His children to have an attitude like Christ. Christ told His disciples *"just as the Son of Man did not come to be served, but to serve, and to give His life a ransom for many." Matthew 20:28 also Mark 10:45 (NIV)*

Are we to serve others and not ourselves first? Yes! That is contradictory to everything the world has taught us since we were watching cartoons as children. But God promises us that if we dedicate our lives to serving others, no matter whether we are led to become a minister of the Gospel, or whether we become the CEO of the largest company on earth, the President of the United States of America, or a cashier in a quick stop store, we will have the most rewarding life a person can have on earth. That life will not always be without pain or difficulties, but God promises that if we rely on His mercy and grace, we will get through anything that life throws our way.

Why would someone do that? How can I serve God and my fellow man at the same time? It is not that difficult. It is a change of our state of mind. Instead of worrying about things like what my vocation will be, or how will I get the kind of car that I want, I will focus on understanding what is God's plan for our life, then dedicating myself to fulfilling that plan. From personal experience I can tell anyone that life is much better when we follow God's plan for our life. It really does not matter what we are called to do in our life, if we dedicate ourselves to serving God no matter how He leads us to do so.

My experience has taught me that in dramatic ways. For years, I was an extremely confident, prideful person who was intent on one thing . . . making as much money as I could and gaining the respect and power that I thought I was destined to have. I went to church, taught Sunday School, sang in the choir, and thought I was a good Christian. But I was never really happy in what I was doing. I was always looking for a way to move up

## Dealing with Being Prideful

the ladder, earn more money, or get in a more influential position where I could show what I thought I was capable of.

Things really hit bottom when I got back from Desert Storm in mid-1991. The company I worked for, AT&T, reorganized my department and the markets that I covered. I was given a different market and quota. By the end of the year, I had reached my quota, and I was expecting to go to our Achievers Club, but at the end of year sales meeting, I was told that my quota was being adjusted where I was at ninety-nine percent, and another sales person who had not made their quota had theirs reduced so that they would have achieved 100% and would be eligible for Achievers Club. I was assured that I would get the raise that I would have gotten had I achieved my quota, but because I had not been active in the sales force for six months before year's end, I would not have been eligible for Achievers Club anyhow!

I told them that was fine, but I also told them that because of getting mobilized for Desert Storm, I had not gotten to go to the 1990 Achievers Club even though I had made my quota, so why not let me go to this year's Achievers' Club to make up for that loss. After all, I was activated for military service in Desert Storm, so was not AT&T somehow obligated to "keep me whole?" As it was explained to me, AT&T was obligated to protect me, and not let me be hurt in any way because I was mobilized. Well, being denied two Achiever's Clubs, and having my work record reflect that I had not made my quota for 1991 because of having it adjusted to give another Account Executive a chance to go to Achievers' Club definitely seemed like I was being almost punished for being mobilized and having to go to Desert Storm. I complained rather vehemently in the meeting that I did not think that was fair and that I felt like I was being punished because I was in the military reserves and had been mobilized for Operation Desert Storm and had been gone for six months. When my management team did not address my complaints to my satisfaction, I and the two managers went outside the meeting and had literally a shouting match where I told them that they were cheating me, and I would not accept their actions. I told them that I was going to complain to the General Manager. They did not take that very well but knew that I was within my rights to do so. At that point I did not care what they thought; I knew that I was condemning myself from future promotions from that point on but I would not let them get away with that type of mistreatment of me when I had certainly lived up to my requirements as an employee..

I appealed that decision all the way to the President of our company but got no satisfaction. At that point, I started searching for another job inside the company. That process went on for over five years during which I probably investigated a dozen or more job openings and none ended up anything that I would prefer over what I was already doing. After the last one, I was at my ropes end. It was around Thanksgiving, and my family and I went on a camping trip to a nearby State Park with the rest of my wife's family.

While my wife and her family were entertaining themselves, I went out into the woods for a walk. There, when I was sure I was out of earshot from everyone, I started praying out loud, very emotional, and quite frustrated. God and I really had a shouting match. I told God that I was tired and just could not continue looking and being frustrated and feeling like I was being punished because of having been mobilized and sent overseas to Desert Storm. I told God that I was not going to look for anything anymore. I told God that I was sorry for my anger, and asked God to take control over my life. I asked God to either move me somewhere where I could not be so stressed out in my work, or if it were His will that I stay where I was, I asked for peace in my heart so that the stress would not continue to cause me trouble at work and in my family because my wife and children were seeing how it was affecting me and that I was very unhappy and could see they were worried about me.

From that moment on, I felt better. I still was not happy at work, but I did not feel the pressure within me to make something happen. I had told God that everything was in His hands, and that I was going to leave everything to Him. I felt less stressed and was not worrying as much about my future. I did not have to wait long for God to show Himself faithful and merciful towards me. In less than two weeks after that conversation with God, my boss called me and offered me a job in Pensacola, Florida where I was the only salesperson in the office, where the market was a well-established market, and where the operation was very low-key. Three weeks after that, another reorganization happened, and now my new boss was a lady in Jacksonville, FL, six hours away from me, who I only saw twice in the entire year I was there.

God proved Himself to me at that point. He was only waiting for me to realize that I was not the person that He wanted in control of my life, that He was, and that if I would only turn things over to Him, He wanted to bless me. Since that time, now nearly twenty-two years ago, I have worried

## Dealing with Being Prideful

very little about my work, or how I would support my family. God has been very faithful, and has continued to bless me way beyond what I deserve, even though at times, almost unconsciously, I have tried to take control back of my life and make things happen, and each and every time I did, the outcome was not nearly what I expected. Then, I would turn things back over to God and He would once again forgive me and show His faithfulness and mercy.

My pride had to be stripped away and I had to learn that when and if I humbled myself before God and allowed Him control of my life, I would be blessed far more than I could have ever dreamed of by trying to do anything myself. Things just are better when we let God control our lives. God has provided the solutions to my problems, even in the cases where I deliberately did something I knew was not in His will because of my pride. Every time I have chosen my way over God's way, it has cost me. Every time I have repented and asked God to take back control over my life, He has shown me mercy and grace, even though I faced some painful consequences for my ways where I had ignored what I knew was God's ways.

Hopefully, from my story above, those reading it who face situations like mine will give God a chance to prove Himself to them. His word promises us that if we humble ourselves and give God control of our lives, His plan will provide us more joy, peace, and satisfaction than anything we can imagine and do on our own.

> *Heavenly Father, thank you for loving me enough to forgive me when I have let my pride lead me away from your plan for my life. Thank you for showing me in undeniable ways that, when given the freedom to do so by me through surrendering my free will to you, that the outcome of what I do in my life is so very much better than when I try to do things "my way" without your input. Thank you for your forgiveness. Thank you for your plan for my life. Please give me the wisdom this day and every day left in my life to let you run my life "Your way!" AMEN*

# Day 10

# Delighting in Our Weaknesses

"... therefore, in order to keep me from becoming conceited, I was given a thorn in my flesh, a messenger of Satan, to torment me. Three times I pleaded with the LORD to take it away from me. But he said to me, "My grace is sufficient for you, for my power is made perfect in weakness." Therefore I will boast all the more gladly about my weaknesses, so that Christ's power may rest on me. That is why, for Christ's sake, I delight in weaknesses, in insults, in hardships, in persecutions, in difficulties. For when I am weak, then I am strong."

2 CORINTHIANS 12:7-10 (NIV)

IN MY EARLY TEENS that I was a little pudgy. But, at the age of fourteen or fifteen, I had a growth spurt where I grew about five inches over one summer. My mother complained about having to buy me new clothes which I outgrew within a few weeks. By the Christmas vacation of that year, I had filled out, gone on a strenuous workout program, and had both slimmed down and grown taller! I was feeling surprisingly good about myself; then I started back to school and realized that as a freshman, I was still relatively small and got pushed around easily by the juniors and seniors. I was determined to end up looking like Charles Atlas, the most popular body builder of that era (Arnold Schwarzenegger had not burst onto the scene yet; he was a young teenager three months younger than me!). I never made it

## Delighting in Our Weaknesses

to that stage, but I was a relatively good athlete. I just always wished that I could have been a little taller, or a little faster, or a little bigger overall. All of us probably wish that we could have been better than we were at some time: better looking, smarter, a better dancer and a better athlete. I do not think during those times, however, that it really crossed my mind about being a better Christian. I certainly do not think that I would have been thanking God for making me like I was. No, I wanted to be better, so I could attain a higher opinion of myself among my peers. Looking back, that was normal. Today, that seems to be an even bigger problem to our youth and young adults today even more than it was in my day. Paul's experience and his lesson in this Scripture totally contradict that attitude as one to be desired.

Paul, in the Scripture verse for this day, was telling the people in Corinth that he had learned to be happy with his weakness. God tells us that it is through our weaknesses that we are made stronger for His kingdom. God's perspective on life is far different from ours. We are in this world, and this is a world where sin, evil, illness, depravity, poverty, and all other forms of human failures are realities. We, by our human nature, are going to focus our attention on what affects us that is real to us in the present. God teaches us that we should focus on what our actions do in preparing us for our Heavenly home. It is only through our being taught about the love of Christ and how God wants us to do things that will lead us to focus on what happens after we die, rather than what happens on this earth. Paul taught us that as we live, we are not to seek attention for ourselves, but only to draw attention to the message of saving grace through God's only Son Jesus Christ.

It seems strange to talk to somebody about being strong in their weaknesses. What does that mean? No-one likes to admit they have weaknesses, especially the guys. Guys are supposed to all be strong, fearless, able to fix anything, cure any hurt, and move mountains. The ladies of today are being told by the world that their worth is measured the same way a man's worth is; by the job she does; how they look, how much they accomplish, and how high they can climb up the corporate ladder. They should be able to do anything a guy can do. Strength and accomplishments are our measurements of worth.

Yet, if we think about things, we should ask ourselves who is stronger and smarter, us or God? Obviously, God is. God, on the other hand, measures us quite differently. When we die and face God to give an account of our lives, we will NOT hear "How much money did you make?," or "How high on the corporate ladder did you go?" Instead, we will stand before God and give an account of our lives. "*And I saw the dead, great and small, standing before the throne, and books were opened. Then another book was opened, which is the book of life. And the dead were judged by what was written in the books, according to what they had done. And the sea gave up the dead who were in it, Death and Hades gave up the dead who were in them, and they were judged, each one of them, according to what they had done. Then Death and Hades were thrown into the lake of fire. This is the second death, the lake of fire. And if anyone's name was not found written in the book of life, he was thrown into the lake of fire.*" Revelation 20:12–15. If we think about it, star athletes, movie stars, politicians, and even some clergy are more focused on furthering their own status and wealth on this earth literally mock those of us who think such achievements are not important. God will judge non-believers and cast them into the lake of fire, but those who belong to Christ (those whose names are written in the book of life) will be judged on what they did for Christ and receive their rewards accordingly.

I have many regrets in my life, but probably the biggest regret I have is that for most of my adult life, I was more concerned with how I got along in the earthly world. It is only in the last few years have I realized how many blessings I missed being concerned with worldly matters, rather than focusing on my relationship and service with Christ. That selfish, worldly view I now understand was so unimportant in terms of my eternal life. Paul writes in Philippians 3:12–14, "*Not that I have already obtained this or am already perfect, but I press on to make it my own, because Christ Jesus has made me his own. Brothers, I do not consider that I have made it my own. But one thing I do: forgetting what lies behind and straining forward to what lies ahead, I press on toward the goal for the prize of the upward call of God in Christ Jesus.*"

The past is gone. I would redo many things in my life if it could, but I cannot change my past. All I can do is try to emulate what Paul says in the scriptures above; put the past behind me and look forward each day to trying to serve Jesus as best as I can with His help while I am still on this earth. Nothing else is more important to me now, but I know I cannot do anything without Christ guiding me and me depending on Christ for the wisdom, strength, and courage to follow His lead. By focusing on God's work that is done through us, especially in our weaknesses, then we are showing the world that God is the source of all of that is good in this world. When we are totally reliant on God for everything in our lives, then whatever we attain, God gets the glory for it, and that draws others to Christ. They see that God blesses us with eternal blessings rather than the worldly attainments which, as He says, will rust, wither away in the fire, and be eaten by moths. *"Do not lay up for yourselves treasures on earth, where moth and rust destroy and where thieves break in and steal, but lay up for yourselves treasures in heaven, where neither moth nor rust destroys and where thieves do not break in and steal. For where your treasure is, there your heart will be also. Matthew 6:19-21, ESV*

Christ said the meek would inherit the earth. When we try to do everything through our own power, we are ignoring what Christ would have us to do and how He would have us to do it. When we are weak in Christ, we know we cannot accomplish anything worthwhile without Him, we then become a tool that He can use, and we start storing up the most valuable treasures anyone can have; a crown of jewels that, when we die, we can lay at the feet of Christ and thank Him for allowing us to be used by Him on this earth.

> Father forgive us when we are boastful and prideful and try to do everything ourselves. Help us LORD to realize that we are weak, so that we can rely on Your strength and guidance to make us strong for you here on Earth." AMEN

*Day 11*

# Dealing with Being Brokenhearted

> The LORD is close to the brokenhearted
> and saves those who are crushed in spirit.
>
> PSALM 36:6(NIV)

IT IS PROBABLY A safe assumption to state that anyone reading this probably has had their heart broken in some way or another in their life. I wish that were not so, but unfortunately, it is. Getting our heart broken is part of life. Dealing with it can be devastating, or it can be a learning experience.

I have certainly had my heart broken many times. Probably my most devastating heartbreak was when I went through my divorce. It was a horribly painful experience, but one that I now know was inevitable. Had I stayed; I am certain that one of us would be dead by now. That is what happens when one does not obey that silent voice warning us about doing something that we know is wrong, and I had heard that voice before I got married the first time but ignored it. That led to one of my life's most painful learning experiences.

This was a time for me where I really let myself wallow in that victim-mentality for an awfully long time ... years! Many a day, I have gone down the road screaming at God "Why God? Where is the justice here? Why did you let that happen?" It was a time where I felt like I had done and acted the way God would have wanted me to act through that whole terrible nightmare, and my ex- acted like a vindictive, mean-spirited person

## Dealing with Being Brokenhearted

doing everything she could to cause me intolerable pain and harm while at the same time I was trying to minimize the pain and hurt between us for my daughter's sake.

Unfortunately, that was all for naught. For years I was bitter and angry, but at the same time, I kept praying that God would somehow give me justice and right the wrongs that I was enduring. That never happened, and I finally came to realize that what I was going through was in many ways my own fault. God tried to warn me, my friends and family tried to warn me, and even my wife's first husband tried to warn me, but I would not listen. I felt like I could fix my wife's problems just by loving her enough. Unfortunately, after sixteen years of trying, after leaving and reconciling with her four times, I had to accept that nothing was ever going to fix that relationship, and the trauma my daughter was having to go through as she watched the marriage dissolve was only going to get worse. I finally had to accept that I had failed in my marriage, as had she, and that there was nothing else I could do at this point but to leave so my daughter might have some semblance of a normal and turbulence-free life. I brought that upon myself because I did not obey His warnings before the marriage to not go through with it. Once I realized that, I could let go of the resentment and anger I felt for my first wife because of the way she treated me, because she was only doing what she thought she had to do and simply could not help herself.

Through prayer and studying my Bible, I learned early on that I had to forgive my ex-wife for what she did. Not because I wanted to, but because God told me that the only way that I could ever survive the pain of that divorce was to realize that He was the only cure for the hurt and hate that filled my heart. I have learned that the forgiving process is not just a one-time thing; it is a daily, sometimes hourly process that we must go through, but that eventually, the reality of God's promises that He will carry us through and heal our hearts is true; we just have to believe His word, and turn it over to Him to heal and sustain us. The forgiveness sustains and heals us, but the loss and pain of separation is always there, we just learn to really forgive by consciously doing it daily through prayer and trusting God when He tells us He will carry us through. He is a faithful God, and I am living proof of the truth of His word.

One of the biggest mistakes people make is when they blame God for what has broken their heart. We ask ourselves "How can a loving God allow this to happen?" Well, to put it bluntly, God is NOT the entity to blame for our problems. Who to blame goes all the way back to the Garden of Eden when Eve ate of the forbidden fruit and enticed Adam to do the same. That act of disobedience was caused by the temptation of SATAN, a fallen angel, who was kicked out of Heaven for rebelling against God. Since that time, every man and woman born on the earth was born with a sinful nature. Satan causes sin, not God. Mankind's own sinful nature is what leads others to break our hearts or allows us to get into situations where we can get our hearts broken.

Blaming God for our problems is putting the blame on the wrong entity. Understanding that, at least for me, answered a lot of questions. The biggest thing I learned when this was pointed out to me was that the things that go wrong, whether we are responsible ourselves, or whether inflicted by others are NOT of God, but are of Satan or by other people's sin nature causing them. God allows things to happen so we can learn a lesson He knows we need to learn, or in the extreme, to break us to the point that we realize the only way we can go to endure what we must endure is to call on Him. There are circumstances and events no human being has the power and strength to endure on our own. That is when it is comforting to know that God is there for those who love and worship Him during the worst times, and that He is that friend who never abandons us, who only wishes to bless us when we rely on Him for all the help we need to get through those times.

God tells us in Isaiah 55:8 (NIV), *"For my thoughts are not your thoughts, neither are your ways my ways, declares the LORD."* We cannot and will not understand the mind and methods that God uses and allows circumstances to happen. That is a fact we must all come to grips with. But when we have the Holy Spirit of God living within us as a Christian, we can have faith to understand this, accept this, and trust that whatever happens, God has our eternal best interests in mind.

If we accept that we are only on this earth for a short period of time as compared to the rest of eternity being spent either in Heaven in fellowship with God Almighty, or in Hell in torment with Satan, then we will understand why God tells us that this time on earth is to prepare those of us who trust Christ as our Messiah to be ready to spend eternity with God. Heaven is our reward for believing in Christ as the Messiah and trying to live our life in a manner pleasing with God. If we accept that principle, then we also will live our lives able to look beyond our broken heartedness because of that faith in Christ and God's promise that we can go through anything and learn from those experiences how to grow and flourish on this earth.

## Dealing with Being Brokenhearted

*(Philippians 4:13 (NIV): "I can do all things through Christ who strengthens me")*

What one does to deal with and get over being broken hearted, is a choice we all must make. We only really have two options:

1. We can choose the victim mentality: We can choose to have a big ole pity party and say poor, poor pitiful me, say that life is unjust, get mad at the world and everyone that we think caused our broken-heartedness, and withdraw into our own little shell. We can stay mad and hurt and focusing our anger and hurt towards those we feel are responsible for our sorrow. This choice will end up poisoning our spirit, making us physically and mentally sick, causing those who love us to worry about us, and in general, doing nothing to make us feel better and help us get along in the world. Or . . .

2. We can choose to recognize that we only hurt ourselves by wallowing in our self-pity and broken heartedness. We must choose to turn the hurt over to God and rely on His strength and promise to carry us through whatever life throws at us. We can realize that God will use this experience to teach us a valuable life lesson and look for what that lesson is and learn from it. Then, we can force ourselves to get up, get out, and get over our pain through focusing on the blessings we have been given, the lesson we have learned, and realizing that even the poorest of us have many blessings to be grateful for. How we handle our pain from our broken hearts is a choice. But the wonderful part of being a Christian is realizing that no matter what we go through in life, we will never have to go through it alone. We always have the Holy Spirit of God living in us and the promise of God that He will never leave us or forsake us in our life. *(Deuteronomy 31:6 NIV) (Be strong and courageous. Do not fear or be in dread of them, for it is the LORD your God who goes with you. He will not leave you or forsake you.")*

Does God sometimes allow us to be "miserable"? While one can find Scriptures that express God's will for us all to live a life of joy, sometimes we as humans will be allowed to be miserable, because it is when we are at our lowest points in life, that is when God really shows up to carry us through those times. It is also through God allowing us to be miserable at times when we are taught that God's grace is sufficient to carry us through the bad periods. He even tells Paul that it is during those time when we are weakest, if we rely totally on God's grace to carry us through, God is faithful to us and that is when we are our strongest for the LORD, because we are relying totally on His grace and strength to carry us through. *And lest I should be exalted above measure by the abundance of the revelations, a thorn in the flesh was given to me, a messenger of Satan to buffet me, lest I be exalted above measure. Concerning this thing I pleaded with the LORD three times that it might depart from me. And He said to me, "My grace is sufficient for you, for My strength is made perfect in weakness." Therefore most gladly I will rather boast in my infirmities, that the power of Christ may rest upon me. Therefore I take pleasure in infirmities, in reproaches, in needs, in persecutions, in distresses, for Christ's sake. For when I am weak, then I am strong 2 Corinthians 12:7–10.*

Paul's assertion completely contradicts the macho assertions of today's "in crowd" that we all must be "all that we can be," or "an Army of One!." While keeping physically fit is indeed a Godly behavior because our body is the temple of the Holy Spirit, that machismo attitude is completely the opposite of what God would have us to act like. Jesus was our role model, and Jesus was a model of kindness, empathy, and love for all, especially the weak. Jesus showed righteous indignation when He saw His Father's temple being turned in to a market for those trying to profit and cheat worshipers coming to the temple to offer sacrifices to God. But in His daily walk, He showed great compassion, was quiet and personable, and always gracious to His hosts. *"Come to me, all you who are weary and burdened, and I will give you rest. Take my yoke upon you and learn from me, for I am gentle and humble in heart, and you will find rest for your souls. 30 For my yoke is easy and my burden is light." Matthew 11:28–30.* It is His wish that everyone spend eternity in Heaven with Him and all the other Christians. When we are broken hearted, we must reach out to God and ask Him to carry us through this pain, and to help us to learn what lesson He wishes us to learn from the experience.

Here are some simple suggestions on how to communicate (pray) to God:

- Be extremely open and truthful when talking to God. He already knows everything about us; everything we do, everything we do not do, our thoughts, our real feelings, and emotions. Lay everything before him that is in your heart and soul

- Start out by saying "thanks" to God for all the good things in your life; itemize them as much as possible. Acknowledge that all good things come from God because He loves us.

- Confess your faults and sins to God. It is lunacy to try and hide anything from the One who created us, who knows our thoughts and everything we do and say. Ask God to help you resist doing those things that are wrong and to help you to live a life more like Jesus did when He walked on the earth.

- Ask God for wisdom to know the truth about your need for Him in your life. We all tend to think we can do anything and everything we need to do to make us happy and successful. Through prayer and God's teachings and blessings, we all learn that God gives us everything; He allows us to make a living, He gives us health to be able to make a living, or if we are unable, He provides for us even when we cannot provide for ourselves.

- Ask God to reveal His plan for your life. It has been my experience when I tried to decide about a path in my life on my own without asking Him for direction, that I totally screw things up.

- Be still at times and listen for God to speak to you. Do not be afraid to ask God to give you a sign to help you know what to do. My experience is that He does just that, and in a way that we know that it could only be His directions, and not our own will. That is one thing that gives me great comfort, and I feel like He will do the same for anyone that simply gives God the chance.

Next, look for Scripture in the Bible that will apply to your situation. You can go to the index or the concordance of your Bible or get on-line. If that does not help call on someone you consider your wise counsel. That person cannot be someone who gets caught up in drama. There are always people in the family who have enough drama to go around.

Day after day, for the rest of our lives, we will struggle against the attacks of Satan. Yes, Satan is a real entity, a fallen angel from Heaven that now seeks to destroy anyone he can so that they will NOT go to Heaven and be with God. In one way or another, Satan is the cause of every hurt or bad thing in our lives. Satan wants everyone to become a slave to his will. If we allow Satan to deceive us, eventually he will destroy our lives on this earth, and for the rest of Eternity. God sent Jesus as the final sacrificial Savior for

## Don't Be a Victim: Choose Victory!

the sins of all mankind. Now, through Jesus' sacrifice, no-one need spend eternity in hell; no-one need have Satan steal their joy while here on earth. Getting our hearts broken is something that happens to everyone; letting that heartbreak continue to steal our joy and ruin our lives does NOT have to happen. Through prayer and faith in Christ and reliance upon God's love, guidance, and provision, we can all overcome heartbreak and live with joy and hope in our hearts.

> *Father, thank you for always being there when my broken heartedness seems to overwhelm me. During the periods where I am brokenhearted, keep reminding me that the sorrow and hurt I feel is NOT what you would have me endure. Help me recognize that with your help, I can overcome that pain and heartbreak, and there is always relief and joy if I will just give my situation to You and trust You to show me the way out. I need to be able to recognize when I need you to guide me. Help me remember to focus on you so that I can be prepared for all that life throws my way, be it good or bad. Let me be an example to others so they will be prepared as well. Thank you because I know you love me. Amen*

## Day 12

## Dealing with Depression

> Answer me quickly, O LORD; my spirit fails. Do not hide your face from me or I will be like those who go down to the pit. Let the morning bring me word of your unfailing love, for I have put my trust in you.
>
> PSALM 143:7-8 (NIV)

WHAT IS DEPRESSION? THE Internet definition I found most accurate is this: *"Depression is a mood disorder that causes a persistent feeling of sadness and loss of interest."* There is psychological depression, and there is clinical depression. Psychological depression relates to emotional problems that we often bring on ourselves because of perceived problems or real problems that we face that seem to overwhelm us. Clinical depression is a medical problem caused by chemical imbalances in our brains that can usually be controlled with medications. Both types of depression cause the same feelings of fear, anxiety, pressure, apprehension and being depressed. Clinical depression almost always requires medication to be put into remission and controlled. Psychological depression can usually be cured without medications through counselling and prayer but can often be so severe that medications are prescribed that improve our abilities to cope and defeat the depression.

Viewing ourselves as victims certainly can be the cause of or make our depression worse; we tend to feel like nothing we do will work for us, that we cannot succeed because all our life circumstances seem to be working against us. We feel like everything we try is going to fail, so we want to give up and withdraw into our own little world where we think maybe the hurting and depression will go away if we can just go to sleep or take a drink or take a pill that can make the depression go away. All of these are false hopes, however, that really never address the root problem of our depression, that is our perception of ourselves as being victimized, treated unfairly, incapable of succeeding at anything, or as someone who is not worthy of anything good in our lives, just to name a few falsehoods.

Depression seems to be looming everywhere in this fallen world. There is depression from not feeling well, from pain, from fear, strained relationships, schedules, problems at work, money problems, and on and on. It is a condition that can be associated with being broken-hearted but is a much more difficult condition to overcome. Naming all the reasons is impossible. Naming the reasons also does not make the problems go away and adds to reasons for being depressed. I am confident that there is no one who has lived on this earth that has never, or will never, suffer from depression in one form and level or another. We see it on television, in the movies, among our friends, our families, and in ourselves from time to time throughout our lives. It is the single most prevalent emotion or mental illness that exists today.

I have suffered with depression over and over during the last forty-plus years. Most of the times, the depression was related to my first marriage and breakup. However, there were other bouts with depression related to my work, my private businesses, and sometimes from circumstances that even I cannot identify; times I just felt depressed and did not know why.

For several years I suffered almost constant depression, doing my best to hide it from the world and especially my new wife. I was prescribed medications to help, but they just turned me into a zombie, so I took myself off them. Each time I really got depressed, I would plead with God, and relief would come. But it was not until I finally forgave my ex-wife and started praying for God to heal her for our daughter's sake that I began to come out of the depression and the times between the bouts with it would be longer and longer.

I also suffered from PTSD (Post Traumatic Stress Disorder). I carried a lot of guilt for decades after Vietnam and all through Operation Desert Storm. I lost three friends in Vietnam. Two of them I had flown with and one was my downstairs apartment neighbor while going through Navigator Training School. I was truly angry when my pilot from my F4 Phantom training was killed. When I found out the circumstances of how he ended up flying Combat Air Patrol (CAP) against his wishes, I became even more angry and frustrated at the way our Federal Government was prosecuting the Vietnam Conflict than before Jeff's death. I felt frustration because I knew Jeff's capabilities, and I knew he requested to not fly CAP because air-to-air combat was not Jeff's strong suite. But because in Jeff's training he had fired an air-to-air missile, he was forced into that mission against his wishes.

I do not mean this bragging, but I was a good back-seater. I knew the systems, the tactics, and I knew the weaknesses and strengths of the pilots I flew with. As a result, at times I had to help them compensate for their weaknesses. I knew Jeff's weaknesses, and I always felt both anger and guilt that I was not in Jeff's back seat on the mission where he was killed. I felt like I probably could have reminded Jeff to stay in formation better and therefore have possibly prevented his being ambushed during a turn where he fell out of position and was ambushed by two MIG 19s.

Another pilot I flew with died when he was on a bombing run, and the airplane started a pull-out, but rolled over and dove into the ground. When I read that, guilt poured over me like lead weights. During a training flight with Jim, he got target fixation and went through the designated altitude required for us to safely pull out of the dive and stay above enemy small arms fire or possibly run into the earth before we could pull out of the dive. I actually had to take the airplane away from Jim and pull it out of the dive because he was so fixated on the target on the ground that he would have run us into the ground trying to get his aim point in the bomb-sight. I should have reported that incident to the training officer, but he asked me not to. He was a Major with thousands of hours of flying time, but no air-to-ground bombing training, and this was his first flight during that phase. I was a First Lieutenant with less than a hundred hours of flying time in the F4, and I acquiesced to his request.

After I heard how he died, it sounded very much like he had continued his attack below the safe altitude again, and he was probably killed by anti-aircraft fire which caused the airplane to crash, also killing his back-seater. My guilt became at times unbearable. I kept thinking that if I had only reported his target fixation that he would still be alive. I told myself that had I told his Instructor pilot, he would either have been washed out of F4 training, or maybe recycled to a later class which would have changed the time he went to Vietnam, and he could not have been killed that day because he couldn't have been there. I carried that guilt for nearly forty years, suppressing it whenever it reared its ugly head, but periodically it would surface causing me periods of depression.

Nearly forty years after Vietnam, the PTSD and some other personal issues drove me to seek counselling at the VA. There, I received therapy that helped me to realize that my guilt was totally misplace. Again, they placed me on medications which dulled my overall mood swings, and eventually I accepted the reality that my guilt was misplaced and that there was no way I could have been there to have an impact. That realization also gave me the confidence to get off the medication. I also realized that, like all of us will someday realize, it just was their time to go. That is when Hebrews 9:27 became real to me (*And just as it is appointed for man to die once, and after that comes judgment*) and I accepted their deaths as God's time for them to come home. I know Jeff was a Christian, so I am assured that he is in Heaven with Jesus, and that gives me great comfort. I do not know if Jim was, but I pray so. He was a good man, and I hope to see Him in Heaven when I get there.

I am convinced that most of the battles with depression, especially with psychological depression, are not going to be won with pills and conventional therapy. Personally, I believe that my depression drove me into God's word and into more intimate prayer, and that is what has continued to give me lengthy periods without depression. God has proven Himself to me repeatedly, and that has strengthened my faith, and my ability to realize that depression is something that I cannot cure, but God can carry me through a bout with depression knowing that God is always there with me and is faithful to sustain me during my down times, and faithful to bring me out of them.

If anyone ever tells you that they have never been depressed, they are probably lying, or are ignorant of what depression is. If anyone tells you that you can just work through depression and beat it on your own, run away from that person as fast as you can; they are either outright lying to you, or they are a self-deluded individual that has no touch with reality. Depression is NOT something one can work through by one's self. I will go so far as to say that it cannot be done. To beat depression, one must have help; help from God, and if necessary, someone that is trained to help a person to recognize that they are depressed, to help identify what the cause of the depression is, and to help the individual to understand what caused the depression, and how they can overcome the illness.

*Dealing with Depression*

A relationship with God is, in my opinion, a fundamental necessity if one is to ever really get over depression, because defeating depression requires one to be totally honest with oneself and with whomever we have entrusted our illness and hopes for overcoming this illness to. That is, in my opinion, much easier to do with God than with any human being on the planet. Why? Because most individuals are extremely reluctant to open themselves up totally to another human being for a variety of reasons; fear of betrayal, fear of embarrassment, fear of others finding out we are going through depression, not wanting to admit weaknesses or feelings of shortcomings or inadequacies, just to mention a few. But since God already knows us better than we know ourselves, it is much easier to open up to God because we know that He already knows what and why we are depressed and is not going to betray our secrets to anyone else.

The Psalms of David are some good examples of prayers in the form of "songs" or free verse poetry, where David literally pours his heart out to God. As one reads them, one can sense David's depression; his seeking God to intervene and help him overcome his depression. The 55$^{th}$ Psalm (NIV) is just one of many where David speaks of his distress:

> *Listen to my prayer, O God, do not ignore my plea; hear me and answer me. My thoughts trouble me and I am distraught because of what my enemy is saying, because of the threats of the wicked; for they bring down suffering on me and assail me in their anger. My heart is in anguish within me; the terrors of death have fallen on me. Fear and trembling have beset me; horror has overwhelmed me. I said, "Oh, that I had the wings of a dove! I would fly away and be at rest. I would flee far away and stay in the desert; I would hurry to my place of shelter, far from the tempest and storm." LORD, confuse the wicked, confound their words, for I see violence and strife in the city. Day and night they prowl about on its walls; malice and abuse are within it. Destructive forces are at work in the city; threats and lies never leave its streets. If an enemy were insulting me, I could endure it; if a foe were rising against me, I could hide. But it is you, a man like myself, my companion, my close friend, with whom I once enjoyed sweet fellowship at the house of God, as we walked about among the worshipers. Let death take my enemies by surprise; let them go down alive to the realm of the dead, for evil finds lodging among them. As for me, I call to God, and the LORD saves me. Evening, morning, and noon I cry out in distress, and he hears my voice. He rescues me unharmed from the battle waged against me, even though many oppose me. God, who is enthroned from of old, who*

> *does not change—he will hear them and humble them, because they have no fear of God. My companion attacks his friends; he violates his covenant. His talk is smooth as butter, yet war is in his heart; his words are more soothing than oil, yet they are drawn swords. Cast your cares on the LORD and he will sustain you; he will never let the righteous be shaken. But you, God, will bring down the wicked into the pit of decay; the bloodthirsty and deceitful will not live out half their days. But as for me, I trust in you."*

Our prayers should be consistent with the plan of God for our lives. This means that we should be asking God to show us a path out of our depression that is consistent with His plan for our lives. Praying for help outside of God's plan will more than likely lead to a "NO" or a seemingly unanswered prayer. We should pray for His spirit to fill our heart and soul. Then the plan of God can unfold in us and diffuse our fear and depression. This takes constant prayer and getting our face in the word. I love to read Psalm 51 and Psalm 143, especially Psalm 51; it is remarkably like Psalm 55 where David is asking God to repair their relationship and to forgive him of his sin with Bathsheba. You can just feel the raw emotion David felt. Please read these Psalms. David wrote this when he was hiding from Saul in caves. He was paralyzed by fear and depression.

There is also clinical depression that may require more intervention such as medication and other therapies. Clinical depression involves chemical imbalances that bring on depression and anxiety more-so than just emotional upsets. That is why it is so important to seek help with your depression either through a good spiritual counselor and/or a good Christian psychologist or psychiatrist if counselling does not provide the results needed. God puts it in people's hearts to want to help others that are depressed. They go through a very lengthy training process which is very effective and can genuinely help people to work themselves out of depression, either with the help of a psychologist, psychiatrist, or therapist, social worker, or trained spiritual counsellor. Please talk to your doctor or a pastor about this if you feel this applies to you and you just cannot shake it or have suicidal thoughts. If other medications or therapies are recommended by your physician, it is still extremely important to keep mentally and emotionally focused on the word of God and in prayer to God, asking for His mercy and grace. One type of treatment without the other is like addressing half of what is needed to receive the peace in your heart that you strive for and what He wants for you.

## *Dealing with Depression*

Father please hear my prayer and pull me from this pit of depression. I can only cope with your help. I need your guidance. I need to feel joy once again. Amen.

*Day 13*

# Dealing with Loneliness and Isolation

"No man shall be able to stand before you all the days of your life. Just as I was with Moses, so I will be with you. I will not leave you or forsake you."

JOSHUA 1:5 (NIV)

PROBABLY EVERY HUMAN BEING at some time in their life feels they are all alone in their struggles with the world. We all feel at times like we are surrounded by people who do not like us, or do not know us and we do not know them, who do not understand us, who like or believe differently than we do, etc. It is like we are alone in our struggles; with no-one we can talk to or lean on to help us overcome the obstacles/challenges we face. Or we truly are in a location where we do not know anybody, where we have no friends or family close by, and are surrounded by people who have different beliefs and values that we do. We are alone in the middle of a crowd of people with no-one to talk to, seek directions or assistance from, or just be a friendly face to talk to. We tell ourselves that talking to anyone will not help because "no-one can really understand where I am . . . what I am going through." Feelings of loneliness and isolation go right along with depression and can often be the source of one's depression.

God spoke the Scripture quoted above to Joshua just after Moses died and Joshua was to succeed Moses and lead the Israelites into the promise land after they had wandered in the desert for forty years. Can you imagine how scary it must have been for Joshua to take the place of Moses? Moses

## Dealing with Loneliness and Isolation

had heard the voice of God and had talked with God one-on-one! He had seen God write the Ten Commandments on the stone tablets on Mount Sinai, then carve the tablets out of Mount Sinai with his flaming fingers. He had heard God tell him that he was going to go back to Egypt, where he had been banished and threatened with death if he ever returned. He had witnessed God's miracles repeatedly as he led the Israelites out of Egypt and to the verge of entering the promised land.

Joshua was faced with challenges that could rival anything most humans today could ever imagine. Joshua had been groomed and prepared by Moses and God for the job of taking the Israelites into the Promised land. Moses was not allowed to enter the Promised land because he had done something to displease God while the Israelites were wandering in the desert. I would think Joshua had to have questioned his own abilities to be able to handle the things he knew Moses did. Challenges like Joshua faced would cause any normal person to question his own fitness or ability to fill the shoes of someone like Moses. But the Scripture quoted at the first of this chapter shows that God promised Joshua that He would never depart from him. But even with that, Joshua faced those same human frailties of loneliness and isolation. All the decisions now rested on his shoulders, and he was responsible for over two million Jews that he was to lead into the promise land.

In today's world, some of the worst cases of feeling lonely and isolated are found in our military veterans. I faced it in Vietnam in 1972, and again when I went to Operation Desert Storm in 1991 and experienced it perhaps even worse when I came home. While in the combat zone, about the only times one had the opportunity to sense the loneliness and the isolation were the quiet times between battles and at night in safe areas. Most of the time, soldiers during a war are constantly moving and busy. We were either preparing for our next engagement or mission, participating in engagements and/or missions, debriefing from engagements or missions, then giving attention to our personal issued items (weapons, uniforms, radios, etc.). It was only when we finished all these requirements and were back in our living quarters alone with time to think did we allow ourselves the luxury of thoughts of home, writing our friends and loved ones, and having those moments when we realized we were lonely, scared, worried about the next mission or engagement, and feeling very alone. Oh sure, we had our fellow soldiers, but with them, we could not communicate like we did to those we loved and who loved us. In battle and on missions, one's thought must be focused entirely on the requirements of the mission; assessing the danger, reacting to it as necessary, watching and waiting for anything to happen, then reacting as necessary with immediate reaction time. Even when not directly engaged with the enemy, one can never relax; always vigilant; always prepared, always squelching any distracting thoughts or talk.

Life in a combat zone is nothing like life back home. Much of the useless bureaucracy of the workplace and civilian life is abandoned and discarded. One does not have much time for contemplating the big worldly problems; one barely has time to figure out what needs to be done in the next few seconds to stay alive. Life becomes much simpler and less complicated. When duty calls, go do it the way we were trained, and hopefully return after the mission and relax for a day or so until the next mission is begun. One learns to live on the edge, because nothing is for sure except the moment being lived right then. This is the cycle of life until one's appointed tour of duty is completed, and the soldier returns home, or perhaps the soldier's race is ended involuntarily.

When we return home, we often find ourselves unable to carry on a normal conversation with our old friends or family. Some subjects our military responsibilities will not let us talk about; some things are just too ugly to talk about; some things a non-combatant could never understand; some things we cannot even bring ourselves to talk about that haunt us. That creates a feeling of being isolated; of being different than the people we are around in civilian lives; feeling like we just do not fit in anymore with the civilian world.

The environment at home is so drastically different from that in a combat zone that it seems almost like a foreign world. We are forced to bottle up our frustrations, our feelings of anger and rage, and to apply a different mindset to getting along with people, doing our civilian jobs, and in our socialization in the civilian world. Coping with our jobs and the old way of handling that responsibility can seem overwhelming compared with the simplicity of doing our military job where we simply conformed with the mission guidelines and do what we must just to fulfill our mission requirements and stay alive.

At times, all of us find it difficult to communicate with those around us for one reason or another. But it is extremely difficult for those individuals who feel isolated from those around them for one reason or another. Whether it be because of combat experiences or other experiences that make us feel isolated and trapped in our own minds, the loneliness and isolation are extremely painful and leave one feeling hopeless and very alone.

## Dealing with Loneliness and Isolation

In times like those described above that I have been through, my only outlet was the communications I had with the Trinity (Heavenly Father, Jesus, Holy Spirit). In those conversations, I could openly share what was on my mind, cry, scream, and ask for help, knowing that whomever I was praying to, if my motives were pure, that God really wanted to help me through my troubles. I have learned that God is the only person/spirit/entity that I can completely trust.

My biggest problems surface whenever I spend too much time talking to God, and not enough time listening to God. It is ironic to me, because all my friends over my life have told me that I am a good listener. Yet with God, I seem to want to do way too much talking and not enough listening.

As I said earlier, I have heard the voice of God two times audibly but have also learned to recognize God speaking to me when I am quiet and listening. A verse of Scripture will come into my head that is pertinent to what I am praying about. I sometimes hear what I call my conscience, but what I believe is really the Holy Spirit like I am talking to myself, telling myself something that I really did not want to hear, but know I am hearing the truth. Sometimes, I hear God acknowledge something that somebody else might be telling me as a truth or a lie. God does answer our prayers, but sometimes the answer might be what we do not want to hear, or the answer might be just a quiet realization of a truth that we do not want to acknowledge, but God does answer our prayers. That is where the trust and the personal relationship with God through faith in Jesus is so precious. Call it a God-given intuition; sometimes we just "know" what God is telling us, what He wants us to do, and what He is telling us NOT to do because that is not a part of His plan for our lives. When we learn to trust God, to believe that He really does want what is best for us and to bless us mightily, we recognize (finally) that we really are never alone, even when we are physically alone, or in a foreign land, or with a group of people we do not even know. We always have that feeling that God is with us, that we can trust Him, and that we are loved immeasurably. With that knowledge, much if not all our feelings of isolation, loneliness, and not fitting in are gone.

> Father, help me to know you are with me in my loneliness times. When it seems no one cares about what I am going through or how bad I feel, please help me to focus on you. You are here with me at my side through everything. Because you are here, I will be strong and very courageous. *Hold my hand and walk me through this loneliness.* AMEN

## Day 14

## Dealing with Shunning Someone or Being Shunned

"Judge not, that you be not judged. For with the judgment you pronounce you will be judged, and with the measure you use it will be measured to you. Why do you see the speck that is in your brother's eye, but do not notice the log that is in your own eye? Or how can you say to your brother, 'Let me take the speck out of your eye,' when there is the log in your own eye? You hypocrite first take the log out of your own eye, and then you will see clearly to take the speck out of your brother's eye."

MATTHEW 7:1–5 (NIV)

I HAVE BEEN SHUNNED many times in my life. It hurts. It can make us feel victimized; like the person shunning us is "picking on us" or treating us undeservedly. No matter what the reason, whether I deserved it or did not deserve it, being shunned is a painful experience. I am certain in my life that I have shunned people, though I can say that I cannot remember doing so from a conscious standpoint; most probably it was done subconsciously, but none-the-less, I am certain that I did so because my conscious tells me I did. I will say that I am ashamed that even in my subconscious mind, I could be guilty of shunning another human being. After being shunned myself, I have always tried to not inflict that hurt on another, and I pray that if I have done so, God will forgive me and heal the hurt of the individual that I shunned.

We should not confuse shunning someone with avoiding someone; those are really two different actions. Avoiding someone does not always involve trying to not contact someone because we do not wish to contact them or must have anything to do with them for whatever reason. Avoiding someone can simply be trying to not make contact because of something we have done, or they have done that we are temporarily embarrassed about and we do not want to face that embarrassment or make them face the embarrassment. There are probably many good reasons for simply avoiding someone, even someone we might consider a loved one or a close friend. Avoidance is usually a temporary situation.

Shunning someone is another act all together. Shunning someone involves making a conscious decision to not have anything to do with another individual, and that act is usually a long-term or permanent decision. While possibly not always the case, the act of shunning another individual usually revolves because of some perceived difference in another human being that we do not want to be associated with.

As a child, often the shunning was subtle, like not being invited to attend a function where all my other "friends" were invited to go to; not being invited or being allowed to join a group that I wanted to be in because I had friends in that group; or being kicked out of some group because I did not measure up to the group's standards somehow, or failing at some task while my friends were passing that task. These and many other reasons resulted in my being rejected for one reason or another either by groups or individuals. Did I deserve some of these rejections? Yes, but the rejection still hurts. And the rejections for reasons that I could not control really hurt. But I have learned from those rejections and have tried to avoid causing others the hurts I felt through rejections.

With so much divisiveness in our nation today, there are a lot of people who are shunning others who we do not like or who we disagree with. And wherever there are people that shun other people, there are people being shunned, and feelings being hurt. Is there any justification for doing so . . . yes and no. The Bible is full of admonitions for people to avoid other people. Readers in Scripture are encouraged to avoid people who have communicable or incurable diseases, who are unrepentant sinners, idolaters, thieves, cheats, adulterers, homosexuals, etc. For one reason, in biblical times, that was the common thinking of men so that the diseases which could not be cured would not be spread among others not infected with that disease. That admonition also applied to those individuals that were born with mental illnesses, and those who developed mental illnesses after birth. Fortunately, modern medicine has done away with the public perception of many diseases and thus eliminated the shunning unnecessarily of sick people. Of course, there are still those cases where individuals who contract extremely dangerous and sometimes incurable communicable diseases where the risk of spreading the disease is extreme and the consequences deadly lethal. But the stigma associated with much of those diseases has lessened the instances of shunning the individual for all the wrong reasons, and has simply replaced that stigma with the realistic reasoning of the avoidance of spreading a disease that could kill thousands, instead of shunning because the person is branded as unclean and unworthy to be loved and cared for like any other human being.

Unfortunately, however, there is still a lot of shunning being done for all the wrong reasons, such as:

- Not looking like the celebrity standard of socially desired appearance (too fat, too thin, being bald, too short, too tall, etc.)
- Not being a part of the "in" crowd at school or work because of their economic or social status in the community
- The social or economic status of their family (divorced, single parent, unwed mother, former prisoner, on public assistance, etc.)
- The category of job one fills (laborer, clerical, janitorial, secretarial, unemployed, fired, crooked politician, bookie, loan shark, etc.)
- Education level one has attained
- Ethnicity
- Religion
- Nationality
- Some sort of physical abnormality (speech impediment, visually impaired; hearing impaired, physical deformity, etc.)
- Political affiliation
- Lifestyle choices

The Bible is specific at time with instructions when we should avoid others. Some of those instances where the shunning needs to occur, however, shed light on the motivations one should examine before shunning another individual. To sum it up in a few simple ideas, I refer to the Scriptures where Jesus instructs his followers on "judging" others. Jesus says that before we judge anyone, we should first judge ourselves, get our hearts and minds right with God, and then try to get our brother or sister that has strayed away from the teachings of the Gospel to repent (admit their faults and ask God to forgive them and to try and avoid repeating those faults again) and seek forgiveness from God. If that brother or sister refuses the first time, then get more friends and brothers in Christ to accompany them back once more to try and get the brother or sister that has strayed to repent and seek forgiveness. If the brother or sister that is sinning refuses a final time, then it is time to leave and as Christ says, shake the dust from the sinner's house off their feet, and then, if contact between the sinner and their Christian brethren occurs, the contact should be a loving but firm call to repentance.

Common sense also must be exercised as we try to decide who we should shun. For instance, if someone trying to kill you, like a radical Islamist extremist-that person should be avoided. A person trying to hold up a bank or a store armed with a pistol should be avoided. One does not deliberately walk into a deadly situation where one's life is in danger unless he or she is a policeman, a soldier, or a healthcare person trying to save another's life. But to shun someone for any of the reasons listed above is just not biblical.

Shunning a person for other than biblical reasons is wrong. It is judging that individual to be unworthy of your company or friendship. Jesus is very direct in his instructions to us when He tells us "*You hypocrite, first take the log out of your own eye, and then you will see clearly to take the speck out of your brother's eye . . ." Matthew 7:5 (NIV) Jesus demonstrated how we are to treat people who the rest of the world deems unworthy of our friendship and love.* When the adulteress was brought before Him, He acknowledged that she was indeed guilty and by man's law, should be stoned to death. Then what did He do? "He challenge\d the accusers: ". . . *let he who is without sin cast the first stone." John 8:7 (NIV)* None of the accusers threw a stone. When accused by the religious leaders of the day that He kept company with sinners, Jesus said to them, "Who is in need of a physician, the sick or the person who is not sick?" Matthew 9:12 (NIV). He said that He came into the world not to condemn the sinners but to save the sinners. Are we any better than Christ? Christ did not shun sinners but taught that we are to try and save the sinners and to love them as Christ loved us while we were yet sinners.

We are all created equal in God's eyes. For us to judge anyone as inferior or unworthy of our love and attention is to basically say that our judgment is better than God's. We are all sinners, worthy of God's condemnation. We should try to remember to look at all our brothers and sisters through God's eyes. Then maybe we will not be so quick to look down our noses at others, but to look at them as someone God loves, and try to love them, or help them come to know Christ as their Savior so they can enjoy the fellowship with all Christians both here on earth and in Heaven. There is only one entity that is fit to judge us, and that is God. We can judge someone's actions and, if necessary, condemn those actions, but to judge another as being an inferior creation is to ignore the instructions of our Creator and Heavenly Father. I for one, choose to not be guilty of that sin. Likewise, we are to forgive those who shun us and try not to repay their unkindness with unkindness of our own. And, if we feel like another person's acts need "judging," we are instructed to first be sure we are on firm biblical ground. (I take that to mean be sure the Scriptures are backing up our judgment, and then even seek the advice of another individual perhaps even wiser than us on the matter before passing our judgment.)

> Father, forgive me if I harbor any hard feelings towards those who, for any reason, shun me. I ask you, in Jesus' precious name to take away any hard feelings that I may have. I ask you to touch the hearts of those that may have shunned me and let them know that I love them, forgive them, and will always treasure their friendship and love. I pray that You will restore in them the faith and courage to overcome their fears so that we may once again fellowship together. And finally, Father, please help me never to look down on others or shun them. AMEN

*Day 15*

# Understanding Repentance and Forgiveness

> For if you forgive men when they sin against you, your heavenly Father will also forgive you. But if you do not forgive men their sins, your Father will not forgive your sins.
>
> MATTHEW 6:14–15 (NIV)

I HAVE USED THOSE terms over the last few days on numerous occasions, so I thought I should spend a little time discussing them and how they relate to not being a victim. It is important for everyone to understand that unforgiveness and unrepentance are two selfish, un-Christian acts that will turn a normally sweet, loving person into someone that is eaten up inside with hate, resentment, jealousy, envy, and spite for others. Unrepentance and unforgiveness are focused totally outward, but they destroy our own insides and our abilities to enjoy the blessings of this life to the fullest. Repentance and forgiveness are two acts that are also essential to become a true Christian.

Repentance is the act of repenting, which is defined by Merriam Webster dictionary as follows: "*To turn from sin and dedicate oneself to the amendment of one's life; to feel regret or contrition; to change one's mind.*" I have had several pastors explain it like this. They explain that repenting of our sins is more than just confessing our sins and asking God to forgive us; it means that we realize we are acting in a way that is displeasing to God, and that realization should break our hearts. It also breaks God's heart because He loves us so deeply. Our repentance makes us no longer want to break God's heart, it makes us want to behave in such a fashion that we honor God, so we ask Him to forgive us and help us live in a fashion that honors Him and pleases Him. It involves a change of heart; a change that perhaps makes us a different person. In many people's lives, the change is so profound that they completely change their behavior patterns that may have existed for decades.

A person eaten up with hate, resentment, jealousy, and envy cannot understand this change. They cannot because they are missing the single most important gift from God that makes such a change possible, the gift of the Holy Spirit that comes to live within us when we accept Christ as our Savior. That gift of the Holy Spirit functions in so many positive ways. For one, He inspired me to realize that I had to forgive the one person that I thought I could never forgive, and to pray for that person to truly open their heart to Christ and receive His love and forgiveness. I had to realize that, as Dr. Rick Warren wrote on the opening page of his blockbuster book *The Purpose Driven Life* "It's not about you!." That means that life on this earth is not all about what I can do for myself, but what I can do with my life to bring people to Christ. It is about showing the world that we were not put on this earth just to satisfy our own wants and needs. We were put on this earth for other purposes, the foremost of which I believe could be described as service to others where that service leads others to believing in Christ as their Savior so they can spend eternity in Heaven with God.

That may sound crazy to someone who has not received the gift of the Holy Spirit through believing in Christ as their Savior, but take it from one that has been through both scenarios, the real joys in life do not come from self-gratification, but from subordinating our own wills to those of our Savior Jesus Christ. The realization that the Creator of everything loved me enough to give His own Son Jesus Christ so Christ could become the last sacrifice to God the Father for every sin of every person ever born is unfathomable to me. Then, after making that decision and actually hearing God speak to me in my mind, which was as real as I hear voices with my ears, and seeing things occur in my life that defy any other explanation than God's intervention in my life are such amazing gifts that now nothing else matters more than trying to live for Him.

Forgiveness is a rather simple concept to explain, but perhaps a much more difficult action to have really happen is to forgive from one's heart. In the Gospel of Matthew, Jesus talks extensively about forgiveness, and perhaps the most important point to stress is this: Unless we forgive others that have harmed us, we will not be forgiven by God where we have sinned against Him. Jesus says it almost exactly that way in Matthew 6:12-15 (NIV): "... *And forgive us our debts, as we also have forgiven our debtors. And lead us not into temptation but deliver us from the evil one. For if you forgive other people when they sin against you, your heavenly Father will also forgive you. But if you do not forgive others their sins, your Father will not forgive your sins."*

There is a lot of discussion over this statement by Christ in his Sermon on the Mount, and the statement by Peter in Acts 10:43 (NIV) *"All the prophets testify about him that everyone who believes in him receives forgiveness of sins through his name.,"* and the one by Paul in Romans 3:23, 24(NIV). *"for all have sinned and fall short of the glory of God, and all are justified freely by his grace through the redemption that came by Christ Jesus."* The arguments back and forth in Christianity are over which condition truly exists, the unconditional forgiveness of sins and saving grace given when one professes faith in Jesus as the Messiah (Acts and Romans verses), or the conditional forgiveness as spoken by Christ in the Sermon on the Mount in Matthew chapter 6?

This is a VERY important point to understand, because it can cause a lot of confusion and appear to present contradicting statements about what is the requirement to become a Christian; is it simply believing in Jesus as the Son of God, the Messiah, or are we required to forgive everyone that has sinned against us AND believing in Jesus as the Son of God, the Messiah. However, the different commentaries seem to agree on an explanation that makes perfect sense even to me.

Jesus is addressing his disciples when He teaches the LORD's prayer, as is seen in verses at the beginning of Matthew chapter five. When He is addressing them with His teachings, He is addressing true believers in Him; He is not addressing the "Gentiles," as he referred to non-believers. So, when He says that we must first forgive those who have sinned against us before our Father in Heaven forgives us, He is talking about the forgiveness of a Christian that, through the sin of unforgiveness, has had their relationship with the Father broken. The forgiveness Jesus is referring to is the restoration of the broken relationship that the sin of unforgiveness has created between God and the unforgiving Christian. He is NOT talking about the forgiveness that is granted unconditionally when a non-believer accepts Christ as Savior and Messiah. That is the type of forgiveness Paul and Peter both state that is given unconditionally through the acceptance of Christ as their Savior. Simply put, we accept Christ as our Savior, we are forgiven of our sins and made Holy in the eyes of God the Father, and we are sealed with Christ for all eternity. But if we do not forgive others who sin against us after becoming a Christian, our relationship with God is broken until we do.

Forgiveness and acceptance into the Kingdom of God comes one way: by believing in Jesus Christ as LORD, Savior and Messiah. Jesus states that very clearly when He says to his disciples "I am the way, the truth, and the light. No man comes unto the Father except by me." Therefore, to simplify this point, we must understand these few points:

1. Forgiveness of our sin requires repentance.
2. Repentance is turning away from our sins; it is recognizing that we have sinned, and then confessing our sins, asking God to forgive us and help us not to sin again. It is actually having a change of heart about the way you want to live your life.
3. Repentance includes asking Christ to forgive us of our sins and to be our Savior and Messiah, and receiving the Holy Spirit
4. Repentance involves trying to live your life in service to Christ and to others.

In Christianity, when one does all the above, that is called being "born again." That is what is pictured during the baptismal service; when a person is dunked under the water, that person's old self is dying to sin, and our new self is raised up out of the water into the newness of life with Christ.

All of this is important to understand, because believing in Christ as our Savior is the single most important act someone will ever make in their lifetime. That single step starts us on our path towards a totally different path in our lives. It opens our eyes to a view of our life on this earth from a perspective we never had envisioned before. Why could we not envision this path before? Because it was waiting to be revealed to us only after believing in Christ and the receiving of the Holy Spirit to indwell us. But once that was done, we now can see that life on this earth really is only a steppingstone, a preparation for a life in Heaven with God the Father, Jesus the Son, and the Holy Spirit. Life on earth is a preparatory event, a training ground where we come to understand that we are so much more than these earthly bodies; we are eternal beings created to spend eternity fellowshipping with our Heavenly Father, His only Son Jesus, and there will be no more pain, no worries, no separation from loved ones, no sickness or loneliness; only eternal joy and worship and fellowship forever with our fellow Christians.

For me, this truth about the true nature of life was so freeing. I no longer feared death; in many ways, I looked forward to it. I learned to forgive, and in fact it made me want to forgive people that I never thought I could forgive. I learned that forgiveness is not a one-time event, because every time someone does another hateful act, we must forgive that act as well. Forgiveness is a learned behavior; it takes intentional determination and a genuine act of love towards people that we once thought were unlovable. I learned to love people that I never thought I could love. I learned to separate what people do from the people themselves, and I learned to realize that when people do bad things, it is because they do not have the Holy Spirit guiding them, revealing right and wrong as God sees it, or because they have a weak moment even as a Christian. I learned to understand exactly how evil SATAN is, that he is a real demon, a fallen angel, and that it is his goal to destroy as many lives as he can. I learned to believe that Hell is a real place where people who reject Christ will spend eternity separated from God. I learned to understand just how awful that feeling of separation from God is. I learned that as a human, I am going to sin because I am a weak person in many ways-that I sometimes cannot help myself-but that when I do, I can go to my Heavenly Father and beg His forgiveness for my weakness and have that relationship with Him restored. I learned that there are Christians out there who want to help me be a better Christian. They, like me, fail at their attempts not to sin continually, just like me, and must beg for forgiveness and restoration just like me. I learned that the only difference between me and the vilest sinner on this earth is one thing: the grace that Jesus provided me by becoming the sacrifice for ALL sin for ALL mankind, for ALL time. And I learned that grace is the most wonderful gift anyone can ever receive. Grace humbled me beyond anything I can ever imagine. I realized that the God of the Universe was willing to sacrifice His only Son because He loved me so much that He knew I could never be righteous enough to earn Heaven. I needed Jesus' sacrifice to wash me of my sins forever so that I could receive the gift of Heaven. As I think of it now, it still just amazes me. The reason I am writing this book is so that hopefully others will read it and understand how precious that gift was and want to receive it themselves. That is my prayer.

## Don't Be a Victim: Choose Victory!

*God, I am so thankful that you reached down from Heaven and bestowed the most amazing gift mankind could ever receive-the gift of grace through my acceptance of Jesus Christ as my Messiah and Savior. God, please help me to always recognize my need to repent of my sins and to forgive those that have sinned against me in the past. In the name of Jesus, I confess to you that I am unworthy to receive your forgiveness, but I do that not because of anything I have done, but because you gave Your son, Jesus Christ, to die on a cross for me, so that I could accept him as my savior and receive forgiveness through the Grace that Jesus' crucifixion and resurrection have provided me. Please help anyone who reads this prayer to open their hearts to Jesus and to accept the gifts of forgiveness, redemption, and grace through Jesus. Help me each day to strive to be more like you so that others may see you in me and come to you as their Savior also. AMEN*

## Day 16

## Forgiving Yourself

So if the Son sets you free, you will be free indeed.

JOHN 8:36. (NIV)

TO GET STARTED I feel I must give a definition of the word "stronghold" from a Biblical perspective. Writer Bill Perkins defines a biblical stronghold as "A spiritual stronghold is a fortress of lies built in the soul." "http://billperkins.com/spiritual-stronghold/!!" It is a belief established and built upon something said by someone trusted which sounds trustworthy, but which is a lie.

What is something you have never forgotten that you said or did that you regret to this day? Let me guess, you have asked God for forgiveness, but cannot forgive yourself. Or you say you forgave yourself, but those thoughts creep back in. At times, those memories can take away your joy and make you question whether you are not a genuine Christian. Also, let us not forget there are people quick to remind you at times of those transgressions from our past that we wish we could forget or correct! With "friends" like that . . . well, let us just say that it keeps us humble!

Those thoughts we cannot let go are strongholds. Those thoughts will make us question our faith and our relationship with God. Those are the thoughts that Satan is using to target our minds to complicate and hinder our relationships with God. Satan puts those thoughts into our minds to prevent a solid relationship with God. And if we do not have a solid relationship with God, we could go back to the sins we were trying to overcome. It is so strange to me that Satan cannot read our minds but can put thoughts into our heads! Have you ever thought to say out loud, "I rebuke you Satan in the name of Jesus"? I will tell you that I do exactly that, and it really does help to shut those thoughts out. I love the verse *"Be self-controlled and alert. Your enemy prowls around like a roaring lion looking for someone to devour. Resist him, standing firm in the faith, because you know that your brothers throughout the world are undergoing the same kind of sufferings. I Peter 5:8–9."* (NIV)

Scripture is the strongest weapon we can use against Satan's attacks. Scripture is God's Holy Word given to us to know how to live while on this earth, what we should value, trust, and cling to through our struggles. It also teaches what is truth and what is false, what to believe and what not to believe as we are bombarded with messages and information daily. Scripture is given by God through divine inspiration to those who have recorded it. Scripture itself confirms this. For example,

> *John 17:17 (ESV) Sanctify them in the truth; your word is truth.*
>
> *2 Timothy 3:16–17 (ESV) All Scripture is breathed out by God and profitable for teaching, for reproof, for correction, and for training in righteousness, that the man of God may be competent, equipped for every good work.*
>
> *2 Peter 1:20–21 (ESV) Knowing this first of all, that no prophecy of Scripture comes from someone's own interpretation. For no prophecy was ever produced by the will of man, but men spoke from God as they were carried along by the Holy Spirit.*
>
> *Revelation 22:18 (ESV) I warn everyone who hears the words of the prophecy of this book: if anyone adds to them, God will add to him the plagues described in this book,*
>
> *John 14:6 (ESV) Jesus said to him, "I am the way, and the truth, and the life. No one comes to the Father except through me.*
>
> *Psalm 19:7 (ESV) The law of the LORD is perfect, reviving the soul; the testimony of the LORD is sure, making wise the simple.*
>
> *Revelation 21:5 (ESV) And he who was seated on the throne said, "Behold, I am making all things new." Also he said, "Write this down, for these words are trustworthy and true."*

## Forgiving Yourself

*John 10:35 (ESV) If he called them gods to whom the word of God came—and Scripture cannot be broken*

The Bible assures to us that through believing in Christ as our Savior and through confession and repentance of our sins, God forgives and forgets our sins. *"If we confess our sins, he is faithful and just and will forgive us our sins and purify us from all unrighteousness. 1 John 1:9." "as far as the east is from the west, so far has he removed our transgressions from us. Psalms 103:12."* Does God actually forget our sins? Yes! Then he adds: *"Their sins and lawless acts I will remember no more." Hebrews 10:17."* So, If God has forgotten our sins, what right do we have to allow the memory of those forgiven and forgotten sins by God continue to haunt us and cause us pain and regrets? We do not! Satan uses our guilt complex to distract us and make us think that we are unworthy of God's forgiveness and therefore of our fellowship with God. In doing so, we allow Satan to hinder our ability to effectively serve the LORD while on earth.

Only by relying on the promises of Scripture, the ability we get through being redeemed by Christ's sacrifices on Calvary, and our acceptance of Him as our Savior can we fight through the guilt and take hold of the promises of Scripture that assure us we are forgiven. Through Scripture, we learn we can rely on God's promises to make us effective servants for Him. That is a promise that each of us should cling to as we "fight the good fight" against Satan and all his attempts to destroy our witness for Christ.

Our faith is strongest when we have a quiet time alone with the Father on a regular basis. Bible study and learning is cleansing to our spirit and necessary for our faith in God. It provides a shield of protection that helps us to resist the enemy.

How many of us see our brothers and sisters making destructive decisions? Let us not judge them but instead pray for them. Many of us have been or could have been in the same position. If we were able to resist, more than likely it was because we had someone praying for us during those trials!

> Dear God, I need to be aware of the spiritual war that exists to harm those I love and myself. I know faith in You is my best defense. Please help me to recognize when Satan tries to enter in my mind and my life. I want to praise You for what You have done to change me. Amen.

*Day 17*

# Dealing with Anger

"What causes quarrels and what causes fights among you? Is it not this, that your passions are at war within you? You desire and do not have, so you murder. You covet and cannot obtain, so you fight and quarrel. You do not have, because you do not ask. You ask and do not receive, because you ask wrongly, to spend it on your passions."

JAMES 4:1-2 (ESV)

I AM THE TYPICAL red-headed stepchild; I have anger issues. I get mad easily and lose my temper. As a child, I was always in fights; in my 4$^{th}$ grade school year, I have been told that I was in a fight three or four days out of every school week in the 4$^{th}$ grade. I got made fun of a lot because I lived with my grandmother who did not have a lot of money. I had to walk to school or ride my bicycle to school all through elementary school because my grandmother had a 1949 Buick with torn seats that did not run very well and was covered with pecan sap which made its green color look motley spotted with brownish black splotches. I remember as an adult when my grandmother was in the nursing home that Daddy had that car towed away to the junk yard. I laughed so hard when I heard about it; Dad said that it had been parked so long under those old pecan trees on our street that it was totally brown. So many leaves and pecans had fallen into the area between the rear bumper and the car body that there was a six-foot pecan tree growing out of that area.

## Dealing with Anger

Seems like I was always mad at somebody; my "friends" would make fun of me because of my curly red hair and freckles; my "friends" made fun of me because I didn't have the most trendy clothes; my "friends" made fun of me because they got Mo-Peds and Motor-Scooters while my grandmother did not even have a recent car. My "friends" who would not help me when the school bullies picked on me.

There are a million reasons that we get mad, this Scripture above tells us that the issues that we fight about are as old as civilization. We covet what we do not have while we covet what our neighbors DO have; we feel we are not loved, are not loveable, and resent those that are loved and are lovable. We are hurt, so our natural defense mechanism is to get mad and hurt somebody so they will feel as bad as we do. But I remember that no matter how many fights I won, I never felt much better after the fight than before the fight; I was only a little more physically damaged than before the fight.

James, the brother of Christ wrote in this passage that we do not have because we do not ask. Is that true? I can sure remember going to bed many nights asking God to please let this girl like me as much as I liked her, but I do not remember that ever happening. I can remember crying myself to sleep because I bragged that my dad was going to buy me a Moped after he told me that he would try but it never happened. The date that this was supposed to happen came and went, and there was no Moped at my grandmother's house. I dreaded having to face my friends; I had told them that Dad was going to buy me one. I was ready for a fight if anybody said anything. Fortunately, I think they were wise enough to know how embarrassed I was, and my friends were truly kind about it.

As an adult, I first saw this passage and it made me mad! Just ask? But then I realized what James was saying. Taken out of context, this verse seems to say that all we must do is ask God for something, and "Poof!," there it will be. But James is speaking of asking not for earthly things, because God tells us that putting our faith in earthly things is only going to end up with us possibly dying rich with world goods, but poor in the treasures that endure; the treasures that God has for us when we die and go to heaven to spend eternity with him there. I was up into my twenties before I read where Jesus promises us that if we seek Him first, He will provide for all our needs. *"Do not store up for yourselves treasures on earth, where moths and vermin destroy, and where thieves break in and steal. But store up for yourselves treasures in heaven, where moths and vermin do not destroy, and where thieves do not break in and steal. For where your treasure is, there your*

## Don't Be a Victim: Choose Victory!

heart will be also . . . *So do not worry, saying, 'What shall we eat?' or 'What shall we drink?' or 'What shall we wear?' For the pagans run after all these things, and your heavenly Father knows that you need them. But seek first his kingdom and his righteousness, and all these things will be given to you as well. Therefore do not worry about tomorrow, for tomorrow will worry about itself. Each day has enough trouble of its own." Matthew 6:19-21, 31-34 NIV*

I began to realize that the person that gets angry is the one that gets hurts the most. Anger is a very destructive, depressing emotion that only serves to fog the mind and heart of the person that is allowing the anger to control him. It rarely hurts the person with whom we are angry unless we verbalize our anger to them. Often, there is no person or thing to focus our anger on; we get angry over circumstances over which we have no control over, over incidents that we could not prevent, and things that we really do not need, but just want, thinking that possessing some object will sooth our troubled souls.

Later in that chapter, James told his us that allowing anger to control us separates us from God and allows Satan to use us for his purposes. Instead, James taught us to turn away from the things of the world, be humble instead of angry, and honor God: "*Submit yourselves therefore to God. Resist the devil, and he will flee from you. Draw near to God, and he will draw near to you. Cleanse your hands, you sinners, and purify your hearts, you double-minded. Be wretched and mourn and weep. Let your laughter be turned to mourning and your joy to gloom. Humble yourselves before the LORD, and he will exalt you." James 7-10*

Anger is tied very closely to pride. Pride is one of the six things that God specifically says He hates! "*There are six things that the LORD hates, seven that are an abomination to him: haughty eyes, a lying tongue, and hands that shed innocent blood, a heart that devises wicked plans, feet that make haste to run to evil, a false witness who breathes out lies, and one who sows discord among brothers." Proverbs 6:16-19.*

Let go of the anger. After all, has being angry ever healed anyone? Has being angry ever brought you satisfaction? I am betting not, based on my own past. It was not until I gave my heart to Jesus and learned the beauty of being humble before God that I began to see the joy and satisfaction that I felt when I submitted myself to God. He then honored me by allowing me to sense his presence and fellowship with Him.

As James said," Humble yourselves before the LORD, and He will exalt you." You can believe that; I personally have witnessed it and lived it.

*Dealing with Anger*

Our Father, please forgive me when I become angry. Come into my heart and purify my thoughts. Cleanse me from my anger and prideful feelings. I humble myself before you and ask you to instill in me the humility of one of your true servants. Let me feel the joy of your presence within me. Fellowship with me, Father, so that I may be a better person and a better witness to my fellow humans." AMEN

## Day 18

# Controlling My Tongue
*Grace-vs-Condemnation*

> Likewise, the tongue is a small part of the body, but it makes great boasts. Consider what a great forest is set on fire by a small spark. The tongue also is a fire, a world of evil among the parts of the body. It corrupts the whole body, sets the whole course of one's life on fire, and is itself set on fire by hell. All kinds of animals, birds, reptiles, and sea creatures are being tamed and have been tamed by mankind, but no human being can tame the tongue. It is a restless evil, full of deadly poison. With the tongue we praise our LORD and Father, and with it we curse human beings, who have been made in God's likeness. Out of the same mouth come praise and cursing. My brothers and sisters, this should not be. Can both fresh water and saltwater flow from the same spring? My brothers and sisters, can a fig tree bear olives, or a grapevine bear figs? Neither can a salt spring produce fresh water.
>
> JAMES 3:5–12 (NIV)

IN THE LAST FEW months, I have read and heard several instances where a young person has committed suicide after being bullied by fellow students. I have seen more stories like this over the last few years than I care to remember. Cell phones, with their text messaging and voicemail provide an avenue of instantly sending out hurtful and insulting messages before having time to think through the impact of what is being sent. The Internet provides access to every form of depravity known to man on display for anyone who want to view it. The Internet and emails provide a path of sending out hurtful, damaging images and messages to anyone anonymously if desired. With all these methods of sending, receiving, and reviewing harmful messages and images at will, the temptation to strike out harmfully can be irresistible for someone who has not been taught a moral code at home which reflects the immorality of using one's words to inflict harm on another human. These failures to instill the proper moral compass to individuals has created a crisis in our nation and the world where humans are led to using the tongue as a cruel, mean, and deadly weapon against others.

This type of human behavior is symptomatic of a world where our focus as humans is totally on self-gratification, rather than the Christ-like behaviors of being motivated to love others more than self and to desiring to serve others more than desiring to be served. The "me" focus drives individuals towards a world where the accumulation of material goods, the admiring and envying friends, and the worldly recognitions are touted as the ultimate measurements of success. The attitude often exhibited by such self-focused individuals is one of doing whatever it takes to attain the worldly goals for which we strive, regardless if that means hurting others to attain those goals. If it means lying or destroying another person to achieve what we want, so be it. The Internet, cell phones, and emails makes that destruction capability far too easy; we can destroy another person's reputation or self-image without ever looking into the eyes of the individual that we are destroying or harming. It gives us a coward's way of being mean and of destroying someone, turning the act into an impersonal, almost anonymous act of incredible destruction and devastation. That just makes it all the easier to be mean and cruel, and that is the act of a true coward.

Not only in the Scriptures quoted above, but all throughout the Bible God speaks through his prophets to warn us to avoid the temptations that the world throws at us and to seek the wisdom of godly people. In the book of Proverbs, there are over twenty references to using the tongue wisely and to warning of the damage it can do if used unwisely. We are encouraged to bless others, not destroy them with our mouths (Proverbs 11:9). We are encouraged not to be the spreader of tales about our neighbors, but instead to keep silent—NOT GOSSIP (Proverbs 11:12–13 (NIV). We are warned that the words of the wicked lie in wait to destroy, but the mouth of the upright person will deliver them (Proverbs 12:6–7(NIV). We are warned that an evil man is ensnared by the transgressions of his lips, but a righteous man will escape from troubles (Proverbs 12:13–14). We are told that the rash tongue cuts like a sword, but the tongue of the wise brings healing; also, that truth lasts forever, but a lying tongue is only for a moment (Proverbs 12:19–20 (NIV).

These are only a few Scriptures that warn and instruct us on how we should use our tongues. I have seen it time and time again in my life; words that were kind and lifted up others were remembered forever and were soothing to one's soul, but words that were cruel and hateful were like the slashes of a sharp knife that leave deep scars on one's soul. And sadly, in the long run, the person who speaks cruelly and untruthfully about another person to make themselves feel better only wounds both. The truly wise person will use their tongue as a tool to lift others up and encourage them to love and follow God, because in the long run, those are the only words that make this world a better place in which to live. Material goods and the praise and recognition gained from harming others will eventually lead only to a life of continually searching for "more," yet never attaining that complete feeling in the pit of their soul that can only be filled by a personal relationship with the Living God. I know this; because I have tried it both ways, and while material success can bring physical comfort, it never fills that hole like the love of God and the knowledge that the God of the Universe, the creator of us all, loves us. That is the true reward on this earth.

I can attest to the truthfulness of what is written above. I have chased material goods, I have focused on attaining success, position, and recognition; I have attained that to a level far above what I ever dreamed I would do in this life. And while the material rewards and recognition have been flattering, that is not what I think back on and remember as the "best" times of my life. The best times of my life are the memories of some of the most insignificant acts to the eyes of the world, but which provided me the memories that last a lifetime. That includes mission trip to Peru where I slept in thatched reed huts, played with native children and heard them laughing almost hysterically over the simplest of games; being asked by the brother of the daughter of the village chief if she could have her picture with her baby made with me; taking a Sunday School class to sing Christmas Carols at a home for adults with developmental challenges; praying for guidance and receiving it from God; seeing my children baptized as Christians; comforting a friend that was dying; holding my mother and dad's hands as they were dying, knowing that they had accepted Jesus as their Savior, and that I would see them in Heaven when I die. Those are some of the moments that I remember as the most significant in my life.

The things that break my heart are NOT the lack of material goods or recognition but are the numerous times I have failed to follow a path that in retrospect was towards where God was leading me, or failed by following the path that in retrospect was NOT what God wanted me to do. I regret not serving God better in my life; I regret not being a better father and husband and friend.

The reason I am writing this devotional at this stage of my life is NOT for money or fame or recognition. I simply want to help people to avoid the pain that I have experienced in my life by not having my priorities straight early in my life. My prayer is that anyone who reads this sentence will simply stop and reflect on their life. Which are the memories that one looks back on with the strongest positive feelings? Which are the ones looked back on with the strongest negative memories? How many of the positive ones were about material gains? How many of the negative ones related to our relationships with our family or with God? We leave this life with exactly what we brought into this life-nothing! The only things that go with us are the things we did that bring honor and glory to God; all else are folly. As the Bible says, "it is appointed once for man to die, and after that the judgment. (Hebrews 9:27 (NIV). The ultimate goal for any person should be that after they close their eyes in death and then open them in Heaven, to hear from Jesus, "Well done, thy good and faithful servant." Remember the old saying" there are NO pockets on a burial shroud."

> *"Oh Father, may I tune my heart to yours so that the words of my mouth would be pleasing unto your ears. Help me always to see others through your eyes so that I may have the same heart for them as You. May my words help others to sense the love that You have for all of us, and may they draw others into a relationship with Jesus as their Messiah and Savior so that they could spend eternity in Heaven with You. Forgive me when my words do not meet those goals and correct my thoughts so that they are pleasing to you. AMEN"*

## Day 19

## Dealing with Guilt

*"There is therefore now no condemnation to those who are in Christ Jesus, who do not walk according to the flesh, but according to the Spirit. For the law of the Spirit of life in Christ Jesus has made me free from the law of sin and death."*

ROMANS 8:1 & 2 (NIV)

FEELINGS OF GUILT ARE one of life's most difficult challenges to overcome. All of us, whether we like to admit it or not, sin against God and our fellow humans innumerable times every day of our lives. It seems like the harder we try to live good lives, the more we seem to fail, which causes us to feel guilty and to feel unworthy of God's love, of God's blessings, and of God's forgiveness. Guilt feelings are destructive to anyone that suffers from them. God does not want us carrying around our guilt. That is why He provided us the forgiveness and redemption from our sins through the sacrifice of His only son, Jesus Christ. *"If we say that we have no sin, we deceive ourselves, and the truth is not in us. If we confess our sins, He is faithful and just to forgive us our sins and to cleanse us from all unrighteousness. 10 If we say that we have not sinned, we make Him a liar, and His word is not in us.* 1 John 8–10 (NIV)

In these verses of Scripture, John the Apostle is telling us that everyone sins. To say that you have no sin is a lie and not of God. But, through Jesus Christ, God's only Son, we have forgiveness of our sins and no condemnation once we confess and are forgiven. Therefore, after confessing our sins and receiving God's forgiveness, to continue to carry around guilt from our sins is wrong. That defeats God's will for our lives by hindering or preventing us from fulfilling our purpose on earth. It also keeps us from receiving all the blessings that God wants to give us through our obedience and fellowship with God.

Time and time again in my own life, I have battled with guilt. I finally realized that Satan was using my guilt feelings to make me feel unworthy and to prevent me from being a blessing to others. Once I realized that, I started learning how to overcome guilt and accept God's forgiveness. Our guilt tells us we are unworthy, makes us compare ourselves to others and overwhelms us at times with feelings of inadequacy, unworthiness, and failure. When we learn to accept God's forgiveness, we overcome those feelings, and open our hearts to be used by God.

A perfect example of trusting God is the example of David and the death of his infant son conceived with Bathsheba. The prophet Nathan came to David and said that because of his sin with Bathsheba, all the LORD's enemies lost respect for him, so his punishment would be the death of the child.

David confessed his sin before the LORD, and when the child became sick, he fasted and stayed in the house lying on the floor of the house and praying until the son died. When he found out the child was dead, he got up off the floor, bathed, put on good smelling oils, and dressed nicely. When he was asked why he did that, he said that he had prayed and hoped that God would spare the child, but when the child died, he realized that he had paid that price, and that nothing he could do would bring the child back. David accepted God's judgment as just and deserved, but also knew that he had paid a just price for his sin and would therefore just have to let it go because holding onto it did no good. God knows our hearts; He knows if we are sincere when we repent of our sins, He knows if we accept the consequences of our sins with the right attitude, and then He forgives us according to our sincerity and His promises to do so through the sacrifice of Jesus on the cross as the ultimate sacrifice for all mankind's sins.

That is how God expects us to approach our sin. We are to confess our sins, accept the responsibility for them, accept the forgiveness of them, and move on, hopefully learning a lesson of the price of sin and the joy of having them forgiven and erased.

Christ wipes our sins away; the Father remembers them no more. *"For as the heavens are high above the earth, so great is His mercy toward those*

## Don't Be a Victim: Choose Victory!

*who fear Him; As far as the east is from the west, so far has He removed our transgressions from us." Psalms 103:11,12(NIV).* The toughest thing to do is to believe and trust God, then press on by allowing God to take us, use us, and make us who He wants us to be. In that trust, in that believing, God gives us the victory over guilt, and the true meaning of happiness.

> Father, I thank you for Jesus' sacrifice so that I may receive forgiveness for my sins. I lay my sins and my guilt before you and ask you to forgive and cleanse me so that I may fellowship with you for eternity. Help me to put my guilt and past behind me so that I may be a better servant and instrument on earth for You to use for your glory and to be a blessing to others. I trust you and accept your gift of forgiveness and redemption through Christ Jesus. AMEN

## Day 20

## Dealing with Lack of Control

"Commit your works to the LORD, and your thoughts will be established . . .
A man's heart plans his way, but the LORD directs his steps."
PROVERBS 16:3, 9 (NIV)

ONE OF LIFE'S BIGGEST challenges is understanding and figuring out how to control ourselves, our moods, our futures, etc. God has given us free will, and that free will is what we use in making decisions about what we do. For a child of Christ and a believer in God's word as given to the prophets, many Christians have come to realize that even though we have free will, our lives are better in every circumstance when we surrender that free will back to God.

Psalms 139 tells us that God knew us and wrote every day that we would live in His Book of Life: *"Your eyes saw my unformed body. All the days ordained for me were written in Your book before one of them came to be." Psalms 139:6(NIV).* That seems to conflict with the idea that we have free will, until we analyze exactly what God is saying here. God tells us that the number of days of our lives are predetermined, but that does NOT mean that He spells out with what each of those days is going to be filled. We have choices; this includes the choice of taking charge of our own lives and doing what we want and think we should do or doing what God has ordained for us to do.

## Don't Be a Victim: Choose Victory!

Every day of my life, I try to remember to ask God to take every step of my day; I ask Him to use me and direct my steps so that I can be a better servant for him. Submissiveness to God, I have learned the hard way, is the only way to find true contentment. Every time I have tried to plan my own path instead of following what my heart told me was God's will for me, I have had to suffer the consequences of the sin that went along with the choices that did not honor God.

Does this mean that if we do not ask God to direct our lives that we may not be successful? Well, obviously, if one looks at the number of successful people in the world who are not Christians then we must draw the obvious conclusion that one can become successful and powerful while never even having heard the name of Christ. But God is telling us followers of Christ that although we may receive material success, fame, and power even if we do not ask God to guide our ways, we will be missing out on even better rewards that would be ours if we did follow His will in our lives. God is not so concerned with our material wealth or our worldly status; He promises us in Matthew 6:33 that if we seek His kingdom and righteousness first, He will provide for all our needs. But God has a higher goal and reward in mind for us. God wants to give us something that we cannot receive without giving God control of our lives; a life full of the peace, joy, and happiness that comes from the personal relationship with our Heavenly Father. Through that relationship, we can receive the contentment that can only be gained by following God's plan for our lives and surrendering our free will to God, so we can fulfill His plan for our life here on earth in preparation for our eternal life in Heaven with Him. Through His word, that is the best choice we will ever make; I promise on the Word of God. The choice is yours; choose wisely.

> Our Father, I am tired of trying to control my life. I surrender that control to You. I freely ask you to take my free will; I do not want it. This day, and each day for the rest of my life, I ask you to take my will and make it yours. Give me the desires of Your heart; and make them the desires of my heart that I may serve you better, both here on earth, and in the life to come in Heaven." *AMEN*

*Day 21*

## Being Able to Endure

For everything that was written in the past was written to teach us, so that through the endurance taught in the Scriptures and the encouragement they provide we might have hope. May the God who gives endurance and encouragement give you the same attitude of mind toward each other that Christ Jesus had, so that with one mind and one voice you may glorify the God and Father of our LORD Jesus Christ.

ROMANS 15: 4-6 (NIV)

LIFE IS FULL OF challenges which requires endurance; determination, and courage to get through. I can remember several instances in my life which required me to endure events which I did not know if I had the strength to endure. The separations and final breakup of my first marriage, the loss of time with my daughter, combat in Vietnam and the separation from my wife and two boys during Desert Storm were all instances where I really had no choice but to endure, even though several times during those most trying times, I cried out to God to just take me home because the pain and heartbreak were more than I wanted to endure. But each time I thought I could not endure or stand the pain any longer, God was always there and carried me through. In the Scriptures above, Paul is telling us that Christ knows what we are going through. The torment and torture He went through during his persecution and crucifixion are beyond human comprehension, both physically and mentally.

## Don't Be a Victim: Choose Victory!

I cannot say for sure, but in my mind, what Christ went through mentally was far worse than the physical pain that He had to endure. The Bible says that Christ was with God in the beginning; He had never endured a moment throughout all eternity without the presence of God the Father and the Holy Spirit. On that cross, when Jesus took on the burden of all the sins of everyone on the planet-those who lived before and those who would ever live after Him, God the father had to turn his head away. Jesus felt alone for the first time in eternity when He cried *"My God, My God, why have you forsaken me? Matthew 27:46 (NIV)"* What must that have been like? For the first time in eternity, Jesus' spirit felt the absence of the presence of His Father's spirit. Try to remember a moment in our lives when we felt alone, overwhelmed with fear, grief, anger, and frustration. Remember how horrible that feeling was? Remember the nervous tension, fear, and almost panic that seemed to overwhelm us? I do. Those were the worst times and moments in my life. But I was still alive, was still working and striving to regain control of my life and holding onto whatever gave me strength to endure and move on. Christ, in His agony cried out to His Father in Heaven. In my own case, I did the same. I cried, pleaded, bargained, and screamed in anger and frustration at God for relief. And He answered, every time. Sometimes it was just with a feeling of peace and determination that came from remembering a Scripture that spoke to my need at that time. At other times, it was some unknown factor that would occur like possibly remembering an instance in the past like what I was going through where I had persevered. Sometimes it was the lyrics to an old hymn or any other song that reminded me that I was not alone and that others had felt the same as I did and persevered. Whatever happened, though, I was able to persevere and survive; eventually, God made everything okay. Even now, as I think about situations that exist in my life that are painful, I have that hope and confidence that God is in control-that He loves me, and that He promises me that if I trust Him, He will carry me through so that things will be better. I have learned through many years of trial and error that I have a source of help that always has my best interest in heart. In Jeremiah 29:11-14 God promises me: *"For I know the plans I have for you," declares the LORD, "plans to prosper you and not to harm you, plans to give you hope and a future. Then you will call on me and come and pray to me, and I will listen to you. You will seek me and find me when you seek me with all your heart. I will be found by you," declares the LORD. . . ."Jeremiah 29:11-14 (NIV)* We need not worry about ourselves, because God has promised us

## Being Able to Endure

that we, who are His adopted children through faith in Jesus Christ as our Savior, have a hope and a future to prosper us. We are not to worry because of that promise. But even during the toughest of times, we should be focusing outwardly on what impact our actions have on others. Remember, God put us here to live out His plan for our lives. That plan is to serve Him and our fellow man in His name. This purpose never changes! Whatever our condition, whatever our blessings or trials, our focus is always to be on how we can still be effective and successful in carrying out God's plan for serving Him. Jesus is the perfect example of that. He is the example we were given by God to follow in good times and in bad times.

On the cross, Jesus' focus was not on Himself. During His torment, His cry was *"Father, forgive them for they know not what they do."* During his ministry, He told His disciples that *"Not so with you. Instead, whoever wants to become great among you must be your servant, and whoever wants to be first must be slave of all. For even the Son of Man did not come to be served, but to serve, and to give his life as a ransom for many."*

Virtually any soldier will tell you that when in a battle, one of the strongest motivating factors for fighting hard is the fear of letting down our fellow soldiers and being the cause of something happening to them. When someone is focused more on the needs of others, it makes doing what we must do much easier. By finding a way to take the focus off what we are going through and looking for ways to help others get through what they are going through, we help ourselves and the other person to endure. If it worked for Jesus, the Son of God, I promise you, as Jesus did, that enduring and finding a way to serve and help others while enduring will produce big dividends here on earth, and in our eternal home with the Father. *"Therefore, since we are surrounded by such a great cloud of witnesses, let us throw off everything that hinders and the sin that so easily entangles. And let us run with perseverance the race marked out for us, fixing our eyes on Jesus, the pioneer and perfecter of faith. For the joy set before him he endured the cross, scorning its shame, and sat down at the right hand of the throne of God. Consider him who endured such opposition from sinners, so that you will not grow weary and lose heart."* Hebrews 12:1–3. These are promises from God that are worth believing in and working toward. God is faithful!

> *"Almighty God, grant me endurance to do what I must to survive and thrive, and show me how I might be able to serve You and others to help them endure their trials as well."* AMEN

*Day 22*

# Dealing with Worry

> "Do not be anxious about anything, but in every situation, by prayer and petition, with thanksgiving, present your requests to God. And the peace of God, which transcends all understanding, will guard your hearts and your minds in Christ Jesus."
>
> PHILIPPIANS 4:6–7 (NIV)

I LOVE THE SONG "Don't Worry, Be Happy" by Bobby McFerrin. It's easy flowing lyrics tell us to not let our circumstances get us down and to just "don't worry, be happy." God tells us over and over in the Bible not to worry. In the Scripture above, Paul is telling us that his faith in Christ gives him the power to do anything required to live out God's plan for his life. Paul seems to have found the secret to go through trials that would destroy most people through his faith in Christ. Do you think Paul worried about himself during these trials? The Scriptures do not indicate that he did. I feel like Paul might have had weak moments at times just like we all do when enduring trials that are scary and unpleasant, but his faith and relationship with Christ carried him through.

Paul was persecuted harshly for his beliefs. In 2 Corinthians 11:23–28, it states that Paul "*. . . As an apostle he was imprisoned, flogged, and many times was near death. Five times he received the forty lashes minus one. Three times he was beaten with rods, once he was stoned, three times he was shipwrecked and for a night and a day he was adrift at sea.*" Paul was eventually imprisoned in Rome for years before he was beheaded outside the gates of Rome. So how is it that Paul could make such a statement and face what he did and not let the worry consume his being? Personally, I think we can find the answers when we look back at who Paul was, what he was before he knew Christ, and who he became after he met Christ. Paul was one of the elite members of the Jewish faith before he met Christ. He was well educated and a zealot who went from place to place and persecuted Christians trying to obliterate them and their faith.

But Jesus had other plans for Paul. On his way to Damascus with a friend to persecute the Christians there, Christ struck Paul blind and reduced him to helplessness. The story is told in the book of Acts 22:1-11:

> *"I persecuted the followers of this Way to their death, arresting both men and women and throwing them into prison, as the high priest and all the Council can themselves testify. I even obtained letters from them to their associates in Damascus and went there to bring these people as prisoners to Jerusalem to be punished. "About noon as I came near Damascus, suddenly a bright light from heaven flashed around me. I fell to the ground and heard a voice say to me, 'Saul! Saul! Why do you persecute me?' "Who are you, LORD?' I asked. "'I am Jesus of Nazareth, whom you are persecuting,' he replied. My companions saw the light, but they did not understand the voice of him who was speaking to me. "'What shall I do, LORD?' I asked. "'Get up,' the LORD said, 'and go into Damascus. There you will be told all that you have been assigned to do.' My companions led me by the hand into Damascus, because the brilliance of the light had blinded me. (NIV)*

That would definitely get my attention. Paul was then taught by Jesus and studied three years before actually beginning his preaching. We read in Galatians 1: *I want you to know, brothers and sisters, that the gospel I preached is not of human origin. I did not receive it from any man, nor was I taught it; rather, I received it by revelation from Jesus Christ . . . Then after three years, I went up to Jerusalem to get acquainted with Cephas (Peter) and stayed with him fifteen days. I saw none of the other apostles—only James, the LORD's brother. I assure you before God that what I am writing you is no lie.* Galatians 1:1-12, 18 (NIV)

Paul was called in a miraculous way. Paul never met Jesus when He was alive. Why then would Jesus call a man like Paul to become one of His disciples? I like to think of it as God picking someone that every Jew knew as a man who had, before his conversion, hated Christianity and its followers with a zeal. If such a man as this can be as radically transformed as Paul was, then it is almost impossible to not believe that his conversion was genuine, and his ministry ordained by Christ himself.

Trying to imagine how Paul felt after encountering Jesus the way he did, whenever he faced the numerous trials that he faced, Paul had the peace that can only come from intimately knowing and believing in Jesus and His promises of eternal life in Heaven through Him. With that kind of faith, Paul's ability not to worry about what the outcome was in any of his trials was made possible. He knew that his path on earth was laid out by God the Father through Jesus Christ, His Son. That is why Paul was able to say with absolute certainty that "I can do anything through Christ Jesus who strengthens me." Paul knew without doubt that whatever he had to endure in this life, Jesus was going to carry him through it and that a glorious after-life in eternity awaited him when his time on earth was done. His focus was not on himself and his future, but on completing the missions that Christ Himself had told him were his purpose in being called. His goal in life was to meet Jesus in heaven and hear *"Well done, good and faithful servant!! . . ." Matthew 25:21(NIV)*

> *Father, thank you that you are with me like the air that I breathe. You feel my pain because you have been there and are able to walk me through. Help me be like Paul, having unwavering faith in Your promises that if my actions are inspired by you, focused on completing Your plan for my life, that I have nothing to worry about. AMEN*

*Day 23*

# Dealing with Fear of Death

"The LORD is my shepherd; I shall not want.2 He makes me to lie down in green pastures; He leads me beside the still waters.3 He restores my soul; He leads me in the paths of righteousness for His name's sake.4 Yea, though I walk through the valley of the shadow of death, I will fear no evil; for You are with me; Your rod and Your staff, they comfort me."

PSALM 23:1–4 (NKJV)

THIS IS ONE OF the more comforting verses of Scripture for individuals that are facing the possibility of death. The 23$^{rd}$ Psalms reflects, according to those who study the Bible looking for the history behind Scripture, the feelings of David as he faced possible death from his son Absalom.

At some point in our lives, we will all face death. Some will face it on a repeated basis, although the probability of death coming is frequently more in the mind of the person than the reality of the situation. That was my case when I flew combat missions as a Weapons Systems Operator in the back seat of the F4 Phantom fighter-bomber in Southeast Asia during 1972.

Before my first combat mission into North Vietnam up around Hanoi, I had a night of extreme anxiety. I just knew in my own mind that I was going to die the next day. We were attacking a troop training area, which happened to be the only anti-aircraft-artillery (AAA) training school in North Vietnam. There were reportedly fifty-plus AAA sites on that school.

## Don't Be a Victim: Choose Victory!

As it turned out, our sixteen airplanes attacked that school, and even though the AAA fire was heavier by far than anything ever seen during World War II over Germany or Japan, all of our sixteen airplanes survived that strike without a scratch, which, in my mind, is only attributable to the grace of God.

Once I fully understood that God already had predetermined the day and time that I was to die, coupled with faith in God, it gave me the ability to let go of the fear and just do what I had to do to survive. Sometimes when faced with illness we can have so much fear and exhaustion that all we can do is to try and survive the moment. But, if we can simply turn our focus to the promises of God and release our fears to Him, our ability to do what we must do to survive is greatly enhanced. God promises us that we can do all things through Christ. Once we face our fear of death and turn it over to God, that fear becomes controllable, and soon goes away.

The 23$^{rd}$ Psalm tells me that even when I am by myself, I am not alone. It tells me that I have a Shepherd, someone who is watching over me, protecting me from the evils of this world that are trying to destroy. Looking back at what I went through in combat, I recognize the truth of His promises. During all of my combat missions, even in the most perilous situations that I faced, I never once was incapable of doing everything I needed to do to make sure that my pilot and I were able to accomplish everything we needed to do to make the mission successful and return home safely.

> Father *help me to trust you so that my fears do not keep me from doing what I need to do to stay alive. Help me with this trust so that I can also be an encouragement to others, including my family. Amen.*

# Day 24

## Dealing with Fear during Unsettling Times

"When you pass through the waters, I will be with you; and when you pass through the rivers, they will not sweep over you. When you walk through the fire you will not be burned: the flames will not set you ablaze. For I am the LORD, your God, the Holy One of Israel, your Savior."

ISAIAH. 43:2-3 (NIV)

As the old saying goes, "Into each life, a little rain must fall . . ." In this sinful, evil world in which we live, there may be one or two people who might say they have never had a rough moment, a tough time, a disappointment, or outright fear brought on by some circumstance in life. But if there are such people, you can bet that they are probably lying. The reasons and the situations are too numerous to try to list, but I think it safe to say that everyone in life will have trials, and somehow, we must learn how to not only survive through those trials, but we must learn how to actually learn from these trials, and flourish. I heard a sermon from Dr. Charles Stanley recently that if we understand why these trials are brought or allowed into our lives by God, then we should be thankful for them. *Consider it pure joy, my brothers and sisters whenever you face trials of many kind because you know that the testing of your faith produces perseverance. Let perseverance finish its work so that you may be mature and complete, not lacking anything. James1:3–5.* Sounds weird to me, but the logic and reasoning behind it made a lot of sense.

## Don't Be a Victim: Choose Victory!

First, it is God's plan to grow us into strong Christians who can be effective servants for Him here on earth. Just as our bodies must be exercised and stressed to become strong, our faith also must be exercised and tested so that we can persevere and become stronger witnesses for Christ. Every job I have had required me to go through very intense, and sometimes incredibly stressful training in preparation for my work assignment. As I look back on my life, I have faced many trials; they include combat in Vietnam, a business bankruptcy during the recession of 1988, commanding troops in a war-zone in Operation Desert Storm, a very painful divorce, and losing loved ones to death and separation. Looking back in retrospect, each of the trials that I went through taught me a life lesson that I needed to learn. These lessons made me a stronger person, but also made me a stronger Christian; in each trial that I have faced, I always leaned on Christ. I remember early in my Christian life hearing sermons and reading Scripture that assured me that Christ was always there, and that by leaning on Him, keeping faith in Him, that I would get through this trial, and be a better man for it. My life is living proof that God is faithful, and that His Word in Scripture is true. We can count on the promises in that word because God is NOT a liar, and always keeps His Word.

In my recent trials, I am still seeing God's faithfulness. I have noticed that in trials, I do not fret and worry as much as I did before. I have come to realize that I really have nothing to fear going through a trial; instead, I immediately start asking God to show me the lesson that He wants me to learn. As each situation occurs, instead of getting really upset and staying that way, very quickly I ask God to help me see the lesson that He is trying to show me. I then ask Him to help me always turn to Him and to trust Him to sustain me as I go through the trial.

The Bible is full of stories of individuals that faced enormous trials, but trusted God and then wrote of the joy they had for which they gave thanks to God after making it through their trials. Being a Christian is not an easy journey in the sinful, evil world in which we live. But with a loving, faithful God, we can have the faith and hope that whatever we face here on this earth, in the end, we will spend eternity in Heaven with Jesus and God the Father, where there will be no pain, no worry, no sorrow, no tears. Personally, I cannot wait until that day comes when I open my eyes and see Jesus and can bow down and worship Him in thankfulness for saving my worthless soul from damnation and eternity separated from Him in Hell.

*Dealing with Fear during Unsettling Times*

*Thank you, God, for your love and strength in carrying me through my life's trials. Help me always to remember that there is a lesson in the trial that will make me a better witness and servant for You here on earth, and that is preparing me for my eternity with you in Heaven. As the old gospel hymn says "All my trials, LORD, will soon be over. I am ready any time you want me LORD. AMEN.*

## Day 25

## Dealing with Our Failures

"Not that I have already obtained all this, or have already arrived at my goal, but I press on to take hold of that for which Christ Jesus took hold of me. Brothers and sisters, I do not consider myself yet to have taken hold of it. But one thing I do: Forgetting what is behind and straining toward what is ahead, I press on toward the goal to win the prize for which God has called me heavenward in Christ Jesus.

PHILIPPIANS 3:12-14 (NIV)

PAUL WAS CONVERTED FROM a Jew that traveled all over the Middle East seeking to destroy Christianity to one of Christ's most prolific and enthusiastic Disciples. He did so through a dramatic episode on his way to Damascus to pursue Christians whereon God struck him blind and let him hear Christ speak.

At that point, Paul realized just how much of his life prior to this time had been lived in sin and how much of a failure he had been in the things pertaining to God. All his life, he lived under the misconception that he was living for God and doing things that would get him into Heaven someday. Now, after Jesus has converted him, he realized how wrong all his whole life had been.

Paul's ministry was mostly to the Gentiles. As he traveled, many times, he saw Christian churches he had established in the Gentile world fall back

## Dealing with Our Failures

into their old behavior before their conversion. In *Romans 2:23–25*, Paul said *"God's name is blasphemed among the Gentiles because of you"* (NIV).

We as Christians are to live our lives so that others see Christ in us and to want to have a relationship with God like they see in us. Being a faithful Minister, either as an individual or as a group, does not mean being a perfect Minister. It only means being a Minister who perseveres, constantly seeks to be more like Christ throughout all the days of our lives in all that we do.

Yet, it is impossible for Christians to live like Christ, that is a sinless life. Why? It is because we are born with a sinful nature and we live in a sinful and fallen world. So, how do we reconcile ourselves to this seemingly impossible task of being like Christ a sinless person, knowing because of our sinful nature we cannot be like Christ? The answer is . . . we cannot. Christ did that for us when He died on the cross and took all the burden of our sins with him to that cross. All we can do is when we fail, recognize our failures, confess those failures, ask his forgiveness, accept his forgiveness, and press on, as Paul says in the quoted Scripture verse above.

If the world sees us differently, it should not see a prideful and arrogant person who judges others from a condemning standpoint. It should see a humble, simple, loving, and forgiving person that tries to emulate Christ as best we can. It should see someone who loves them despite their shortcomings, because Christ loves us despite our shortcomings. It should see itself except for one difference, a gratitude that is born from Christ dying for our sins so that we can spend eternity in Heaven instead of burning in hell for all of eternity. It should see someone that loves Christ and is so grateful to Christ that they want others to know their Christ in a compulsive and desperate sense out of gratitude for what He has done for us. It should see someone that is not judgmental of a person's status or relationship with God but as someone who, except for having Christ as their Savior, would be just like them.

When someone criticizes Christians as being hypocritical because they do not live like Christ but look like the rest of the world, our reply should not be condemning to them. Instead, we should give them an analogy something like this one that our minister gave us:

"Just because someone plays Beethoven terribly, that does not mean that Beethoven was not a great composer. And just because someone does not live like Christ, does not mean that Christ is not worth following or is not a good example." One does not become a Christian and then automatically never be a sinner again.

When one becomes a Christian, a person simply learns to recognize his or her own sin, repent of that sin, thank God for that forgiveness, and try harder every day and every minute of every day to live more like Christ. Living life is hard enough without carrying around all the burdens and failures that are inevitably going to be part of every human's life. The ONLY way to make it through this life on earth without carrying around this burden of our failures and sins is to let them go! Jesus forgives us of our sins and has removed the burden of them from us through His death on the cross. By sharing that good news to our friends in the proper way, we can be used by Christ to help save others from having to spend eternity separated from Christ in hell.

> *Father help me to let go of my past failures. Help me to realize that it is wise to learn from my failures, and to realize that the lessons I have learned from my failures are ones for which I will always be grateful. Forgive me when I let the memories of my failures hold back from continuing to "press on" through them and strive to fine new opportunities which I can use to glorify your name. Amen.*

# Day 26

# Dealing with Envy/Covetousness

"Therefore, putting aside all malice and all deceit and hypocrisy and envy and all slander, like newborn babies, long for the pure milk of the word, so that by it you may grow in respect to salvation"

1 PETER 2:1-2

"THOU SHALT NOT COVET *thy neighbor's house, thou shalt not covet thy neighbor's wife, nor his manservant, nor his maidservant, nor his ox, nor his ass, nor any thing that is thy neighbor's.*" This is the 10th Commandment given to Moses by God. Though it is last in the list we should not think it any less important for us to obey. Envy and covetousness are at the root of most of the world's problems today. Just listen to the commercials on radio and television; they are designed to make us want something that we do not have, or something that someone else has.

Envy or covetousness is not just wanting more; it is wanting what somebody else has. It is wanting someone else's car, home, job, airplane, success, recognition, wife, or husband, etc. Harboring envy in one's heart destroys one's soul.

Everybody wants "more"; more money, more cars, more fame, and recognition, more of everything. But that is NOT what God wants for us. It is the desire of our Heavenly Father for us to NOT focus on desires of this world, but to seek after His will for our lives while we live on this earth. *"No one can serve two masters. Either you will hate the one and love the other, or you will be devoted to the one and despise the other. You cannot serve both God and money."* Matthew 6:24. He promises us that if we pursue fulfilling His will for our lives, He will provide us the desires of our hearts. *"Take delight in the LORD, and he will give you the desires of your heart. Commit your way to the LORD; trust in him and he will do this:"* Psalm 37:45

It would be a serious mistake and a misinterpretation of David's intent in writing this to take it out of context and look at it like a wishing well promise. David is not telling the reader that simply by loving and following God that we can then just wish for anything and God will grant that wish. God is not the genie in a bottle.

Instead, David is telling the reader that by devoting oneself to serving God and looking to God for our joy, God will then give us the desires of our heart that match His plan for our lives. David is telling us that we cannot look to the world for the source of things that give us true joy, because we live in a fallen world and much of what the world offers us is only a temporary satisfaction. The world tells us that the more worldly desires we attain, that we then should seek the next shiner, faster, fancier widget, or the more self-indulgent luxury or fantasy that comes along and creates in us the envy and covetousness to step up and grab that brass ring.

The secular, material world is full of people trying to seduce and lure us into wanting more and more of everything they are selling. But God is telling us throughout His word that it is folly to allow ourselves to be lured into that envy and covetous world.

> Heavenly Father, thank You for Your Word that shows us the path to true joy and satisfaction on this earth. Create in me a heart that seeks only Your will for my life. Give me the wisdom to make following Your plan for my life my only goal while I am here on earth, then please give me the courage to follow that plan. In Jesus' name I pray this! AMEN

*Day 27*

## God Promises Us Hope through Jesus

"For I know the plans I have for you, declares the LORD,
plans for welfare and not for evil, to give you a future and a hope."

JEREMIAH 29:11

I REMEMBER THE ASTONISHMENT I felt when I first heard a sermon based on this Scripture. I was well into my adulthood, and I was stunned! That was the first time in my life that I knew that God had a plan for my life. I knew God called certain people to be ministers, but it never dawned on me that God had a plan for each of us that followed Him. At that same time, it started making sense to me why I had so much trouble finding contentment in my life.

This is probably one of the most quoted Scriptures in Christendom today, especially when it is taken out of context and flaunted by the prosperity preachers of today who promise you that God will give you all the riches and blessings you desire based on this Scripture. This is NOT what this Scripture is saying. *"This is the text of the letter that the prophet Jeremiah sent from Jerusalem to the surviving elders among the exiles and to the priests, the prophets and all the other people Nebuchadnezzar had carried into exile from Jerusalem to Babylon."* Jeremiah 29:1 The Israelites has lost their promise of entry into the Promised Land and had been taken captive into Babylon by King Nebuchadnezzar. God had allowed this to happen because the Israelites had disobeyed God and disregarded the warnings from His prophets.

This is a promise to Israelites in Israel that after seventy more years in exile, God would honor His promises to the Israelites to deliver them back to Jerusalem. It is an indicator of the character of God. It is an indicator that God is a just God; it is an indicator that when individuals or nations ignore the warnings of God from prophets or Scriptures, that there are repercussions that will come from ignoring the word of God. It is also an indicator that God is a loving and forgiving God because He tells the Israelites that they will prosper even while in captivity if they keep His commandments, and that if they are faithful to do so for the next seventy years, they will be forgiven and restored out of captivity back to Jerusalem.

For these reasons, this is still a vibrant and living Scripture of encouragement. It tells us that our God loves us unconditionally, even though we may be sinners, and that He is ever willing to forgive us and to restore His loving relationship with us upon our repentance and asking of forgiveness. When we look at the promise to prosper us, we must look at it in terms of God's vision for us where He tells us to store up for ourselves treasures in Heaven, where they will not rust or rot; eternal treasures that are promised to give us joy that nothing on earth can really compare to; joy that is from God for all eternity *"Do not lay up for yourselves treasures on earth, where moth and rust destroy and where thieves break in and steal, but lay up for yourselves treasures in heaven, where neither moth nor rust destroys and where thieves do not break in and steal. For where your treasure is, there your heart will be also."* (Matthew 6:19–21). We may prosper here on earth materially, or we may not. If we do, it should be a gift that we realize is from God, and we should use those gifts to encourage others to follow Jesus, and not just to satisfy our own material desires. If we do not prosper materially, we can rest in the promise that God will supply the needs of all His children.

If God did nothing else for us, that promise of eternity in Heaven would still be the best thing that ever could happen to us. But God does not stop there; He tell us that He has a plan for our lives; a plan which does not harm us but provides for all our needs and more blessings on top of that. James, the brother of Jesus tells us of that: *"Don't be deceived, my dear brothers and sisters. Every good and perfect gift is from above, coming down from the Father of the heavenly lights, who does not change like shifting shadows.* "James 1:16–17

## God Promises Us Hope through Jesus

Paul, when he is writing to the Philippians, says this: *"I have received full payment and have more than enough. I am amply supplied, now that I have received from Epaphroditus the gifts you sent. They are a fragrant offering, an acceptable sacrifice, pleasing to God. And my God will meet all your needs according to the riches of his glory in Christ Jesus. "*

> *Oh God, thank you for Jesus' sacrifice and the hope that gives me of eternal salvation and life in Heaven with You. Thank you for your encouragement in this Scripture where you demonstrate your infinite willingness to forgive our failures and restore our relationship with you. Thank you for letting us all know that you have an individual plan for each of our lives; a plan which is designed to give us earthly joy beyond measure as we serve you in the way you have designed for us. We love you, Father and praise your name for the loving, wonderful, benevolent Father that you are. In Jesus' name, AMEN.*

*Day 28*

# Is Illness/Suffering "Punishment" from God?

The man said, "The woman you put here with me—she gave me some fruit from the tree, and I ate it." Then the LORD God said to the woman, "What is this you have done?" The woman said, "The serpent deceived me, and I ate." So the LORD God said to the serpent, "Because you have done this, "Cursed are you above all livestock and all wild animals! You will crawl on your belly and you will eat dust all the days of your life. And I will put enmity between you and the woman, and between your offspring and hers; he will crush your head, and you will strike his heel." To the woman he said, "I will make your pains in childbearing very severe; with painful labor you will give birth to children. Your desire will be for your husband, and he will rule over you." To Adam he said, "Because you listened to your wife and ate fruit from the tree about which I commanded you, 'You must not eat from it,' "Cursed is the ground because of you; through painful toil you will eat food from it all the days of your life. It will produce thorns and thistles for you, and you will eat the plants of the field. By the sweat of your brow you will eat your food until you return to the ground, since from it you were taken; for dust you are and to dust you will return."

GENESIS 3:12–19

## Is Illness/Suffering "Punishment" from God?

WHEN SOMEONE BECOMES SICK, is that someone being punished by God? We all sometimes feel that way, do we not? The Scriptures above tell us that through Adam and Eve's sin, sin and condemnation entered the world. It is evident from the Scripture above that God did punish Adam and Eve. Through them, all mankind since then God punished for our sinful nature. When we were children, did our parents not punish us at times when we misbehaved? I know mine did. Is it not therefore reasonable to believe that in His infinite wisdom God as our Heavenly Father will use both punishment and discipline towards people to accomplish His plans for mankind? His use of punishment is rather obvious when we look at God's actions towards Sodom and Gomorrah (Genesis 19:1-29). Again, in the book of Exodus (chapter. 32), when Moses was on Mount Sinai receiving the Ten Commandments on the stone tablets, many of the Israelites became impatient and forced Aaron to make for them a golden calf idol for them to worship, God became angry and told Moses that as punishment He would blot out their names from His book and punish them *The LORD* replied to Moses, "Whoever has sinned against me I will blot out of my book. *Now go, lead the people to the place I spoke of, and my angel will go before you. However, when the time comes for me to punish, I will punish them for their sin." And the LORD struck the people with a plague because of what they did with the calf Aaron had made. (Exodus 32:33–35)*

Dr. Woods Watson, Pastor of Senior Adults and Pastoral Care Ministries at First Baptist Church of West Monroe, Louisiana, has written a brief overview of the topic of "SUFFERING." With his permission, I have included that overview below. It gives twelve ways that suffering is used in the Bible to accomplish God's plan for mankind:

## Suffering

*One of the most troubling mysteries in life is suffering. How do we make sense of suffering? Thankfully, the Bible is not silent and does not sidestep the issue. The word, "suffering" is used 53 times in Scripture and the verb, "suffer," is used 49 times. The following presentation categorizes those uses and includes some other relevant Scripture as they help us to recognize the ways of God in suffering.*

1. *Suffering is the result of living in the fallen world—God made the world perfect, but this is not the perfect world that God made. It is fallen and*

cursed. Tragedies and disasters happen here. People die. God is ultimately in control, but He allows bad things to happen in this cursed world. Genesis 3:16–19, 2 Kings 13:14; Ecclesiastes 2:17, Psalm 90:3–10; Matthew 4:24; Acts 7:11; Romans 8:22

2. *Suffering is the result of spiritual warfare*—There is an unseen battle taking place vying for man's soul. Suffering may occur in the skirmishes between good and evil. God allows this war to occur until He eventually brings Judgment with its final resolution. Job 2:13, 30:16, 30:27, 36:15; Acts 9:16; Romans 5:3; 2 Corinthians 1:6; Philippians 1:29; 1 Thessalonians 1:6, 5:9; 2 Thessalonians 1:5; 2 Timothy 1:8, 12, 2:9; Hebrews 2:10, 10:32, 13:3; James 5:10; 1 Peter 1:6, 2:19, 4:12; Revelation 1:9, 2:101

3. *Suffering is the result of the evil deeds of others*—Other people also do bad things to other people. God gives mankind free will to do great good or to do great evil. Genesis 16:5, 41:52; Exodus 3:7; Deuteronomy 26:6, 28:53, 55; Nehemiah 9:9; ; Ezra 4:13; Psalm 22:24, 42:10, 55:3, 107:10, 119:50, 119:153; Isaiah 14:3, 54:4; Daniel 6:2; Acts 5:41; 1 Peter 2:20, 3:14, 17, 4:15–16, 19

4. *Suffering is the result of the judgment of God*—God steps in to bring judgment or discipline on people. The suffering can be a result of the judgment. Even innocent people can suffer when God judges the guilty because they are in close proximity or are related to the guilty. Genesis 4:15; Numbers 5:24, 27, 14:33–34; 2 Kings 14:26; Job 24:11; Jeremiah 14:13; Lamentations 1:12, 1:18; Ezekiel 23:49, 36:7, 15, 30, Joel 1:18; 1 Corinthians 3:15, Jude 7; Revelations 2:22

5. *Suffering is the result of the work of redemption*—Jesus suffered great pain to take our place as the sacrifice for our sins. He suffered so we would not have to suffer. Isaiah 53:3, 10–11; Matthew 16:21, 17:12; Mark 8:31, 9:12; Luke 9:22, 17:25, 22:15, 24:26, Acts 1:3, 3:18, 17:3, 26:23, Hebrews 9:26

6. *Suffering is the result of one's own foolishness or sin*—God gives us freedom to choose; sometimes we choose foolishly or sinfully and suffer the consequences of those choices. Proverbs 9:12, 11:15, 22:3, 27:12; Isaiah 47:8; Galatians 6:7

7. *Suffering is the result of the need for God's healing*—When people hurt, they feel their need for God. God will allow people to suffer in order that

## Is Illness/Suffering "Punishment" from God?

*they will realize their need for God. Matthew 8:6, 15:22, 17:15; Mark 5:29, 5:34; Luke 4:38, 14:2; Acts 28:8*

8. *Suffering is the result of sacrifice for another's good*—Acts of compassion and other deeds of goodness for others often call for sacrifice that can be painful. That suffering can be vicarious when the suffering is done on another's behalf. *John 15:13; Romans 12:10; Galatians 4:19, 5:13; Ephesians 4:2, 32,*

9. *Suffering is a reflection of God's character*—God understands our suffering because He Himself suffers. *Jeremiah 15:15; Hebrews 4:14–16*

10. *Suffering is the requirement to prepare for personal growth and future rewards*—Suffering can develop us in good ways if we respond positively to it. Also, future rewards in heaven are tied to suffering. *Romans 8:28-29; 1 Corinthians 3:11–15, I Corinthians 3:15:58, 2 Corinthians 1:3–11, II Corinthians 4:7–18, James 1:3–5*

11. *Suffering is a reasonable aspect of identifying with Christ*—Jesus indicated that our suffering is a direct result of His suffering. Persecution comes in many forms, but it is the result of Christians' identification with Christ. *Matthew 10:22, Matthew 24:9, Luke 9:23; John 15:18, 2 Corinthians 11:23–29, Philippians 3:7–11,*

12. *Suffering is realized to be a mystery*—Some suffering we will not completely understand. God may one day reveal why it has happened and why it has happened when it did. In the meantime, we will wrestle with various aspects of this mystery. *Isaiah 55:8–9; 1 Corinthians 13:12*

When we contemplate who God is (e.g., He is the Creator of everything; He is Omniscient (knows everything), Omnipotent (all powerful), Omnipresent (present everywhere, always). We realize that God can do anything He chooses. He can bless us, curse us, punish us, rescue us, condemn us, or save us. He is a sinless God (He defines sin as He wishes), and a just God (He will keep His promises and be consistent in the way He blesses, condemns, saves, and curses). Thankfully, God has given us in the Bible of what He expects from those who follow Him. God gave mankind thousands of years to be justified according to the laws He gave us in the Ten Commandments and the Laws of Moses, but mankind was unable to follow those commandments, falling over and over into sin and worshiping other Gods. God knew what it would take for mankind to be reconciled to Him, and that was a Messiah; a Savior, a spotless, sinless, Holy Sacrifice that would provide a manner for sinful man to have their sins forgiven so that they could be reconciled and have fellowship with a righteous God. Jesus became that sacrifice. He voluntarily stepped out of His role as a part of the Trinity in Heaven to become the sacrifice on earth that would give sinful man a way to be forgiven of their sins and spend eternity in Heaven with God the Father, Jesus the Son, and the Holy Spirit, the three-in-one Godhead.

When we are born, we are born with a sinful nature. If we are fortunate enough to be born into a Christian environment where we are nurtured, taught about God, Jesus, and what it takes to be forgiven of our sins and go to heaven, then we have a lot to look forward to. But even in those circumstances, humans are going to sin. In every circumstance, we are taught that sin always has consequences. Those consequences are chosen by God and are chosen to either teach us about the sin/consequence sequence and try to help us not to be so sinful or to "get our attention" and punish us in such a fashion as to make us think twice about whether that sin was worth the punishment.

Unfortunately, there are also people in this world who are just evil, mean, despicable humans. There will always be this type of people on earth until Jesus comes back to take his followers to Heaven in the end times. We have seen these people in every generation, from Genghis Khan to Ivan the Terrible, Hitler, Tojo, Stalin and Mao, the world has always had tyrants and maniacal villains out to subjugate the rest of the world to their whelms. In biblical times, there were numerous rulers that persecuted the Israelites, where God intervened and either directly punished and destroyed Israel's foes, or used leaders from the Israelites themselves to crush their enemies. Punishment in those circumstances would seem appropriate for God to use so that the enemies of the Jewish people would learn that the Jewish people were being protected by a God more powerful than any of the false gods that they worshiped. But as Dr. Watson says above, Suffering ". . . is realized to be a mystery!" Since we are not God, we need to realize that suffering will come into every life, including each of ours. When it does, we need to look at the circumstances and ask ourselves "OK, God, I realize that you are allowing this suffering for a reason. What are you trying to teach me?" If one is a Christian, then God is allowing suffering somehow to make us a more useful agent of service to Him and to help us fulfill His plan for our lives. If one is not a Christian, the suffering could be allowed to draw that soul towards believing in Jesus as their Messiah. The reasons are God's alone, and we may never really understand why we or our loved ones

## Is Illness/Suffering "Punishment" from God?

suffer. At least when we are followers of Jesus, we can genuinely know with conviction that God is working on us to draw us closer to Him and to make us more effective servants of our LORD.

God loves mankind enough and wants us to be able to defeat Satan and sin so that we can spend eternity in Heaven with Him *"For God so loved the world that He gave His only begotten Son, that whoever believes in Him should not perish but have everlasting life" John 3:16*. Reach out to God when troubled; do not turn from God, but run to God! Trust Him, even when you do not understand why or for what you are trusting Him, but just trust him. *"Now faith is the substance of things hoped for, the evidence of things not seen." Hebrews 11:1*

> Our Father, thank you for sending Jesus to Earth to provide we sinners the way to overcome the condemnation of our sin so that we may spend eternity in Heaven with you, where there is no pain, no suffering, no tears, and no sadness. Forgive me my sins, accept me into your kingdom. Heal me out of your mercy from whatever is ailing me, if it can be Thy will, but if not, please use my illness on Earth to help others to come to know you as their Savior." AMEN

## Day 29

## Who or What Is Your God?

"And God spoke all these words: "I am the LORD your God, who brought you out of Egypt, out of the land of slavery. "You shall have no other gods before me. "You shall not make for yourself an image in the form of anything in heaven above or on the earth beneath or in the waters below. You shall not bow down to them or worship them; for I, the LORD your God, am a jealous God, punishing the children for the sin of the parents to the third and fourth generation of those who hate me, but showing love to a thousand generations of those who love me and keep my commandments.

EXODUS 20:1–6

WHEN JESUS WAS ASKED which of the Ten Commandments was the most important, this is what he said: *"Jesus replied: "'Love the LORD your God with all your heart and with all your soul and with all your mind.' This is the first and greatest commandment. And the second is like it: 'Love your neighbor as yourself.' All the Law and the Prophets hang on these two commandments." Matthew 33:36–40*

God is a jealous God, and does not condone His highest creation, we humans, to worship anything more than we worship Him. Yet, at some time(s) in our lives, every human violates this most important commandment by putting something ahead of Him as our priority in life.

*Who or What Is Your God?*

This is the first and most important of the Ten Commandments that God gave to Moses on Mt. Sinai. He rather emphatically tells us that there is only one God, and that is the God of Israel, the one God who made all things, created the heavens and the earth, and everything that crawls, walks and runs on it, flies above it, or swims in the waters on it. Notice verses three through five: The warning God gives mankind against worshipping any other gods is strong! So, why is it that in this world today, people worship so many different gods? I imagine it is because they really do not understand that they are doing exactly that!

In Matthew 6:24, Jesus says this: *"No one can serve two masters. Either you will hate the one and love the other, or you will be devoted to the one and despise the other. You cannot serve both God and money."* God does not allow a divided loyalty; either God is #1 in your life, or He is not, and your loyalty is divided. In other words, if anything is more important to someone than their relationship with and service to God, then they are worshipping another god (money, fame, prestige, recognition, power, etc.) ahead of the one true God. God rejects that *"These are the words of the Amen, the faithful and true witness, the ruler of God's creation. I know your deeds, that you are neither cold nor hot. I wish you were either one or the other! So, because you are lukewarm—neither hot nor cold—I am about to spit you out of my mouth. You say, 'I am rich; I have acquired wealth and do not need a thing.' But you do not realize that you are wretched, pitiful, poor, blind and naked."* Revelation 3:14–16.

God does not accept second place in our lives, and who can blame Him. He created everything. He is the source of everything good and needed in our lives. Most importantly, He sacrificed His only Son Jesus Christ as the ultimate sacrifice for the forgiveness of all of mankind's sins forever! He gave each one of us the privilege of spending eternity in Heaven forever where there is no pain, suffering, crying, or need. Every need is met, every joy is experienced . . . forever!

When I stop and think about what God has done for mankind, I realize just how small His demand is from us so that we can experience Heaven forever. Simply put, we need to humble ourselves before our creator, ask Him to forgive our sins, believe the Jesus is God's Son, the promised Messiah, and ask Jesus to be our own personal Savior. Once that is done, at least for my part, my priorities in life changed completely. I no longer cared about becoming famous, or being a great corporate leader, or anything other than striving every day to make serving Jesus my top priority in life.

## Don't Be a Victim: Choose Victory!

St. Paul understood this when he said in his letter to the Philippians,

> *"But whatever were gains to me I now consider loss for the sake of Christ. What is more, I consider everything a loss because of the surpassing worth of knowing Christ Jesus my LORD, for whose sake I have lost all things. I consider them garbage, that I may gain Christ and be found in him, not having a righteousness of my own that comes from the law, but that which is through faith in Christ—the righteousness that comes from God on the basis of faith. I want to know Christ—yes, to know the power of his resurrection and participation in his sufferings, becoming like him in his death, and so, somehow, attaining to the resurrection from the dead.*
>
> *Not that I have already obtained all this, or have already arrived at my goal, but I press on to take hold of that for which Christ Jesus took hold of me. Brothers and sisters, I do not consider myself yet to have taken hold of it. But one thing I do: Forgetting what is behind and straining toward what is ahead, I press on toward the goal to win the prize for which God has called me heavenward in Christ Jesus. All of us, then, who are mature should take such a view of things. And if on some point you think differently that too God will make clear to you. Only let us live up to what we have already attained*
>
> *Join together in following my example, brothers and sisters, and just as you have us as a model, keep your eyes on those who live as we do. For, as I have often told you before and now tell you again even with tears, many live as enemies of the cross of Christ. Their destiny is destruction, their god is their stomach, and their glory is in their shame. Their mind is set on earthly things. But our citizenship is in heaven. And we eagerly await a Savior from there, the LORD Jesus Christ, who, by the power that enables him to bring everything under his control, will transform our lowly bodies so that they will be like his glorious body."* Philippians 3:7–21

Being completely honest with my readers, I must confess that this is a sin I struggle with daily, along with worrying. Daily, I still fight the struggle to keep serving God as my top priority. Thankfully, God knows that I, and every other human, while on this earth will continue to sin. But I can truthfully say that my heart's biggest desire is to serve God and spread His love and forgiveness to everybody I can reach. God knows I still must work and meet the demands of the world, but those are now what I consider stumbling blocks on my path of service for Jesus. I deal with them as I must, and I eliminate them as I can. I truly want nothing any more than to serve my God however He allows so that I can bring the saving grace of salvation

## Who or What Is Your God?

through Jesus to as many people as He allows and makes a path for me to do so. Nothing matters more to me than when I stand before Jesus in Heaven to hear Him say "Well done, good and faithful servant!"

> Heavenly Father, where I fail to keep service to you as my number one priority, please forgive me and help me to correct those sins of commission. Thank you, Jesus, for your sacrifice. Please help me daily to serve you in as many ways possible, to keep my relationship and service with you as my number one priority in life and bring you all the glory! AMEN

*Day 30*

# Where Your Treasure Is, There Your Heart Will Be . . .

"Do not lay up for yourselves treasures on earth, where moth and rust destroy and where thieves break in and steal; but lay up for yourselves treasures in heaven, where neither moth nor rust destroys and where thieves do not break in and steal. For where your treasure is, there your heart will be also."

MATTHEW 6: 19-21

WE LIVE IN A materialistic world. Everything we see on television and the movies today seemsto focus on how well off someone is materially. Celebrities today are glorified for how beautiful or handsome they are, what type of clothes they wear, what type of fancy cars they have, and who has the biggest house, yacht, or private jet. And yet, we hear every year about how these people, who supposedly have "made it" in life, are destroying their lives and the lives of those that surround them by either trying to escape the realities of their lives, or by killing themselves. The Bible warns us that focusing our desires on material goods is dangerous and foolish. *"For the love of money is a root of all kinds of evil. Some people, eager for money, have wandered from the faith and pierced themselves with many griefs." 1 Timothy 6:10*

Most all of us, except for people like Bill Gates, Warren Buffet, and a lot of the elected politicians today, have faced and, on occasions, continually

*Where Your Treasure Is, There Your Heart Will Be . . .*

face financial difficulties. However, in the Scriptures above, Jesus told people to keep their financial conditions in the proper perspective. Remember that life is more than just possessions, money, houses, cars, jewels, savings, or retirement plans. These are earthly "things," which we did not have when we came into this world, and we will not take with us when we leave this world. As my loved ones have told me; ". . . there are no pockets on a burial shroud!"

Jesus advised us to focus instead on storing up treasures in Heaven. How do we do that when every day we are bombarded with advertisements on television, radio, and in print telling us that unless we have the latest and greatest of everything in society, then somehow we are missing out on life's finest and best experiences? The answer to that question really is a simple one: focus our attention elsewhere. To do that takes developing a character trait that is quite uncommon today, and something that advertisers and promoters do not encourage individuals to exercise: SELF-DISCIPLINE!!

We as individuals need to recognize that every form of advertisement is designed to make us act in a way that someone else is telling us is best for us. These advertisements and commercials are designed to make people think the way that these advertisers want us to think, and NOT the way that is possibly best for us. They are mind manipulators and character shapers. They intend to convince as many people as possible to spend their money on the products and services that they sell. These manipulators have little regard for whether any of us really can benefit or really need what they are selling! We need to realize that. We need to have the self-discipline to not let our minds be manipulated. Instead we must continually ask ourselves questions to determine what is best for us as individuals and our families in the long run. We need to get back to the basics when we look at what material goods and services we really need and should want. More importantly, we need to start focusing on how we can use whatever material goods and services God provides us to help others come to a saving relationship with Jesus Christ so that we, and they, can spend all of eternity in Heaven after our time here on earth is over. News flash! No-one leaves this earth with anything more than exactly what they brought into it, which is nothing! And after we die, the only thing that will matter when we face the judgment of God, will be whether we have accepted Jesus Christ as our Savior, and what we have done while here on this earth to help others come to know Christ as their Savior. *"But He has appeared once for all at the culmination of the ages to do away with sin by the sacrifice of Himself. Just as people are destined to die once, and after that to face judgment, so Christ was sacrificed once to take*

## Don't Be a Victim: Choose Victory!

*away the sins of many; and he will appear a second time, not to bear sin, but to bring salvation to those who are waiting for him." Hebrews 9:26–28*

All of us need to come to the realization that much of our life is manipulated and controlled by what others tell us we should want, feel, and value. It comes to us through what WE allow into our minds through what we watch, read, and listen to. God has given us a plan for our lives and all the guidance we need to make the best life we can have while here on this earth in His holy Scriptures. It is up to us to decide how we will live out our lives. We decide whether we will let the materialistic world manipulate and define who we are and how we will act, or whether we will let our Heavenly Father, who created us and has a plan for our lives, to give us true contentment and purpose for our lives while on earth, and will allow us to store up treasures in Heaven where they will bless us for eternity. Me, I choose God's plan! I have tried the other way, and I am much more content, happy, and blessed when I allow God to lead and direct my life. I encourage everyone to do the same.

> *Our Father, I am tired of the struggles associated with trying to control my life. I choose to not let this materialistic world tell me who I should be, what I should want, and what I should value and do with my life. I surrender that control to You. I freely ask you to take my free will; I do not want it. This day, and each day for the rest of my life, I ask you to take my will and make it yours. Give me the desires of Your heart; and make them the desires of my heart that I may serve you better, both here on earth, and in the life to come in Heaven."* AMEN

## Day 31

## When I Die . . .

> "My frame was not hidden from you when I was made in the secret place, when I was woven together in the depths of the earth. Your eyes saw my unformed body; all the days ordained for me were written in your book before one of them came to be."
>
> PSALMS 139:15-16, NIV

PSALMS 139 HAS BEEN described as the most beautiful and important of all the Psalms. It declares the omniscience, omnipresence, and omnipotence of God. These verses state emphatically that *"all the days ordained for me were written in your book before one of them came to be."*

Simply put, God has it pre-ordained that I will live a certain number of days, and then I will die. There is little I can do to change that date and time unless I fall under the deception of Satan and allow the evil one to convince me to take my own life.

This Scripture tells me that everybody has a date and a time that they are supposed to die. Therefore, my worrying about whether I was going to die on a combat mission or whether I am going to die from some illness that I get is truly a waste of my time. And, frankly, my experiences in combat in the Vietnam conflict convinced me of the truth of that.

If there is one thing that combat really showed me, it was that when it is your time to go, you will go, and if it is not your time to go, you will not go. I flew through concentrations of AAA fire, with SAMs (Surface To Air

Missiles) fired at us, and MIG aircraft attacking us that I did not believe a gnat could fly through without being hit, and yet as many as twenty-four aircraft flew through those attacks without a scratch. Yet, on other missions, I saw individuals killed on the lowest possible threat environment one could ever face. I saw situations where the odds of the aircraft getting hit were millions to one, yet one bullet hit the airplane, killing the officer in the back seat of that F4 Phantom. I heard many tales of similar circumstances; tales of surviving under conditions that everyone around them dies, but miraculously they survive. Tales of others dying when there is no logical explanation or reason that they died, except that the Scriptures do not lie; when it is your time to go, you will go. Death now is something to which I can look forward. I cannot say that I look forward to the act of dying, but even that really causes me no great concern because of all the progress that has been made with hospice care and keeping people comfortable in their last battle on earth. But in conversations with preachers, friends, and even loved ones before they passed, I have come to realize that even the act of dying can be a great opportunity to demonstrate one's faith in the love and mercy of our Heavenly Father. Somehow, I have come to realize that God can even use the act of dying as an opportunity to demonstrate to others one's faith and trust in our loving Heavenly Father and our Savior Jesus Christ. So now, when I wonder about how I will die, I simply ask God to allow me to use that last act here on earth as a way to encourage others that will have to see me go through that. I want God to use that experience to draw others to Him and to Jesus. I just pray that I have that courage and strength to do that when the time comes.

I take great solace in those promises of Scripture. From the time I realized that God has my life in His hands, because I gave it to Him to do with as He chooses, that the fear of death has not been a part of my life. Now, whenever I think maybe I might die, like when I have had to have major back surgery, I just simply tell God that His will be done, because I know that if this is the time I must die, then so-be-it. I know where my next life will be, because I believe the truth and promises of His Holy book. I will close my eyes in death and open my eyes in the presence of God in Heaven. I will not be sick, I will not be hurting, I will not be sad, and I will be rejoicing in the presence of God, my Father, and I have the promise of a happy reunion with my loved ones in Heaven. I revel in the truth of Paul's words, when he declared *"Oh Death, where is your sting; Oh Hades, where is your victory?"* 1 Corinthians 54:55.

## When I Die . . .

*"Oh God, forgive me when I let my fears of death steal the joys of living in this world you have given me. May I spend however many days you have ordained me to live in thankfulness for what bounty you have provided, and in awe of the beauties of your creation."*

*Day 32*

# Hearing What God Has to Say to Us

> "My sheep hear my voice, and I know them, and they follow me.
> I give them eternal life, and they will never perish,
> and no one will snatch them out of my hand."
>
> JOHN 10:27–28 ESV

> "That which was from the beginning, which we have heard, which we have seen with our eyes, which we looked upon and have touched with our hands, concerning the word of life—the life was made manifest, and we have seen it, and testify to it and proclaim to you the eternal life, which was with the Father and was made manifest to us—that which we have seen and heard we proclaim also to you, so that you too may have fellowship with us; and indeed our fellowship is with the Father and with his Son Jesus Christ. And we are writing these things so that our joy may be complete. This is the message we have heard from him and proclaim to you, that God is light, and in him is no darkness at all. If we say we have fellowship with him while we walk in darkness, we lie and do not practice the truth. But if we walk in the light, as he is in the light, we have fellowship with one another, and the blood of Jesus his Son cleanses us from all sin. If we say we have no sin, we deceive ourselves, and the truth is not in us. If we confess our sins, he is faithful and just to forgive us our sins and to cleanse us from all unrighteousness. If we say we have not sinned, we make him a liar, and his word is not in us."
>
> 1 JOHN 1:1–10

## Hearing What God Has to Say to Us

IF ANYONE EVER TELLS you that God does not speak to people anymore, I am here to testify to you that they are telling a bald-face lie! God does speak to those who are followers of Jesus Christ. He speaks to us in multiple ways: The primary way that God speaks to Christians is through His written word. In an earlier chapter, I gave examples of how the Bible is the word of God, written by eyewitnesses to the things observed and the words said by God either through His prophets of old, or by the disciples of Jesus who followed Him for three years while he was on the earth teaching and healing. The disciple Paul was taught by Jesus through revelations where Jesus spoke directly to him and Paul relayed what Jesus taught in the thirteen books of the New Testament that he wrote.

Skeptics have been trying to disprove the Bible ever since it was first written, yet to-date, no-one has ever been successful in doing so. Exactly the opposite has been the outcome; in over twenty-eight thousand archeological excavations, nothing has ever been found to disprove the Bible, but plenty has been found to support what it says.

Jesus also speaks to us through other Christians. In my own case, many times I have had had questions about something, or been in a situation where I was trying to make a decision on some matter and had a Christian friend that I would seek counsel from who had just the Scripture verses I needed to hear that gave me the answer I was seeking. Many times, I have been sitting in church pondering something, or had an issue on my mind and have the preacher's sermon that day be exactly the answer to what was on my mind.

God also speaks to us through circumstances which occur where there is no logical explanation other than God directly intervening on our behalf. I can think of at least three instances in my life during a financially difficult situation when it looked like I would not be able to meet a payment, an unexpected check would arrive to meet that need. Once it was back pay from a promotion in my work, once it was an unexpected payment from an insurance company from a subscriber savings account that I did not even know existed, and once it was a refund from an overpayment on a credit card that I did not know I had made. In each case, the answer seemingly came "out of the blue." Skeptics call them "coincidences," but I have come to believe there is no such thing as a coincidence in the life of a Christian, only the pure unmerited grace and blessings of a loving heavenly Father.

Another way that God speaks to Christians today is directly to us through hearing His voice audibly or in our dreams. That has happened

## Don't Be a Victim: Choose Victory!

twice to me, and I have described both instances earlier in this devotional. There is no doubt when those things happen, and there is also no doubt what one is to do when that happens. One obeys, because when God speaks like that to a believer, we know without doubt that to do what God is saying to do is going to provide the best possible outcome for the believer. I can testify to that, because there have also been instances where I chose to NOT do what God was telling me to. I either let doubt creep in and cause me to question whether or not I was really hearing God, or because I simply let pride and arrogance convince me that what I wanted to do was the best choice. Inevitably, my choice was a huge disaster.

There are many documented cases where pastors and individuals have heard God's voice. Many additional individuals testify of visits to Heaven where they died from an accident or illness and were sent back by Jesus for one reason or another. There are too many of those instances to rationally believe they are all made up. Plus, as a believer, I would be too afraid to say something about encountering God if it really did not happen. Most believers would NEVER do that out of the fear that somehow it might hurt the effort to bring everyone to a saving grace of Jesus. I, for one, would NEVER say anything untrue about communicating with God.

Finally, I think God speaks to us through music. Some of the most wonderful moments where I felt the closest to God were when I was worshipping Him through music. David experienced the same sensations, and he wrote about them in the Psalms. Music frequently provides us a way to express to God that which we would not normally know how to say on our own. I remember during some very difficult times in my life where I would hear a song, perhaps for the first time, that addressed the very emotion that I was battling and told me what I should do. For example, the lyrics to a song by Selah called "Press ON" described what I would say was my exact mental and emotional condition at the time, and encouraged me to just "Press ON," to keep my eyes on the future, to not let the circumstances of my life at that time bring me down.

All I can testify to with absolute certainty is my own experiences communicating with God. I believe that God has spoken to me twice audibly; once in a dream while I was in Southeast Asia that woke me up, and once while praying about a decision about a mission trip. Both times I received an answer regarding a major theological question where I sought not my own will but was looking for guidance from God as to what His will for me was. I genuinely believe I heard the voice of God through the Holy Spirit guiding me.

> *Heavenly Father, thank you for the privilege of being called Your son; a privilege that you give freely to those who accept your offer of eternal salvation through your son Jesus Christ. I freely admit that I deserve nothing but condemnation from you because of my sinful nature. Yet, because you love me, you accept me, forgive me, sanctify me, and bless me. I look forward to each time I hear from You, and I beg you to let me do so more often. Accept my praises and gratitude and forgive me where I fail you. In JESUS precious name, I pray! AMEN*

## Day 33

## God's Grace Is Sufficient in Every Situation

> "But he said to me, "My grace is sufficient for you, for my power is made perfect in weakness." Therefore, I will boast all the more gladly about my weaknesses, so that Christ's power may rest on me."
> 2 CORINTHIANS 12:9 (NIV)

MAYBE YOU CAUGHT THAT this verse was one of the verses I used in an earlier devotional discussion. However, to me, God's grace through Jesus Christ is the most miraculous gift we receive through believing in Jesus Christ as our personal Savior. Paul is telling his followers that His grace is enough for Paul to handle and function even though he (Paul) was suffering from an ailment that he called "a thorn in his side." Paul suffered throughout his ministry. Yet, even from jail, he did not waiver, exhibited joy, and ministered to all with whom he came into contact. How did he do that . . . it was through grace!

So, what is God's grace? According to the Merriam Webster Dictionary, here is how it is defined with reference to religion:

- unmerited divine assistance given humans for their regeneration or sanctification
- a virtue coming from God
- a state of sanctification enjoyed through divine grace

## God's Grace Is Sufficient in Every Situation

Grace is what Jesus provided by going to the cross. All of mankind can experience eternal life in Heaven by believing in Him as their Savior, their Messiah, the promised one from God. This promise is not just for Jews, but for everyone; Jews, English, Spanish, French, black, white, oriental, native Americans, Arabs, Latinos . . . every human being has that opportunity to choose salvation through Jesus. Jesus through His sacrifice on our behalf has paid the debt for all of us which frees us to go to Heaven where we will spend eternity with God.

No person can earn entry into Heaven by being a "good person," by doing good. Likewise, no-one can earn God's favor. It is truly through grace that we receive blessings from God.

> *But because of his great love for us, God, who is rich in mercy, made us alive with Christ even when we were dead in transgressions—it is by grace you have been saved. And God raised us up with Christ and seated us with him in the heavenly realms in Christ Jesus, in order that in the coming ages he might show the incomparable riches of his grace, expressed in his kindness to us in Christ Jesus. For it is by grace you have been saved, through faith—and this is not from yourselves, it is the gift of God—not by works, so that no one can boast.* Ephesians 2:4–9 (NIV)

It really goes against our human characteristics to accept that we are not totally in control of our souls, our livelihoods, and our future. The world tells us to "be all that you can be"; that we control our own destiny, and in truth, we can. Following Christ, believing in Him as our Savior, believing in his gospel as what is best for us to use to live our lives by, goes against everything that the world tells us we should do. But any Christian that has done as the Bible says and turned their lives over to Christ to guide them will inevitably realize, after God shows Himself and we actually give Him control over our lives, that by doing so, we will receive blessings far greater than anything this world has to offer.

God has revealed Himself to me. No, I have not seen God, but I have heard Him speak spiritually to me, and I have sensed His direction in my life. When I followed that direction, an indescribable peace, joy, and anticipation came over me. What thrills me even more that even as I write this, the peace in my spirit almost overwhelms me. I wish I could describe it, but my vocabulary is not large enough to find the proper words. The tears in my eyes are tears of joy; there is a smile on my face that a chisel could not

Don't Be a Victim: Choose Victory!

remove. My heart feels at peace, and I am full of anticipation of feeling like this for all eternity.

I believe after talking with other Christians that the true gift of grace is simply being reassured by God showing us in ways that can only be attributed to His presence and actions on our behalf. This is the best gift anyone can ever receive. Nothing I have ever experienced that the world has to offer can compare to the knowledge that the God of the Universe, the Creator of everything, loves little insignificant me enough to allow me to sense His presence in undeniable ways. God has done that by letting me hear His voice in my head, and hear His directions in my head (all, by the way, because of ardent prayer over a lengthy period). Those instances left me with a hunger and anticipation that is indescribably the best feeling I have ever known. I just cannot wait for the next time.

Just lately, God has revealed Himself to me in additional ways that thrill me as well. By inspiring me to write this devotional, God has led me to do more research and to read my Bible more. It is hard to explain, these days as I read my Bible, read commentaries and life experiences from others relating to Scripture that I read, I feel more and more connected to my LORD. The hunger to learn more, to understand Scripture better, to see Scripture's application in my daily life better, and to share all these exciting and fulfilling experiences make me hungry for more, and grateful for each day that I have to study and experience God's revelations and blessings through studying His word. I pray that everyone that reads this will give God a chance, because I can tell you from personal experience, there is nothing on earth that can compare to the experiences of connecting with God and getting to know Him better. It makes me wish that everyone on the earth would experience it and receive that same joy.

When life seems to overwhelm us with its ugliness; when we get frustrated with our job, our government, our enemies, do not despair. Sit quietly with your Bible and read God's reassuring words in the Psalms, in the Sermon on the Mount, in Jesus' promises to His disciples. Walk out on a clear night and look at the beauty of the stars as they twinkle in the sky. Look at a baby smiling at its mom or dad, or as it giggles hysterically in the joy of living. Listen to beautiful, peaceful music, read the lyrics to beautiful hymns like Amazing Grace, The Old Rugged Cross, Love Lifted me, etc. Smell the roses, lilies, orchids, and tulips. Watch puppies play with unconditional love. All of these are God's creations and gifts. The beauty of His creation is incomparable, and it is ours for free. Enjoy these gifts and sit

*God's Grace Is Sufficient in Every Situation*

in the peace and grace of your God, and humbly say "Thank you, LORD." That pleases your Father in Heaven, and sooths the soul.

> Our Father, I give my life to you; I give you my free will; I give you permission, and I beg you to take control of my life and direct me so that I can be the best possible servant and ambassador for you while I live on this earth. Forgive me when I fail you; set my feet on the right paths back to you. When I fail you, extend your grace to me so that I may repent and once again have life's most precious gift, that fellowship with you." *AMEN*

*Day 34*

# God Is Faithful

"No temptation has overtaken you that is not common to man. God is faithful, and he will not let you be tempted beyond your ability, but with the temptation he will also provide the way of escape, that you may be able to endure it."

1 CORINTHIANS 10:13 (ESV)

IN THIS SCRIPTURE VERSE, Paul is telling the Corinthians that Satan is always tempting us; trying to make us doubt God's faithfulness to us or His love for us, but that God is not the kind of God that just leaves us to Satan's abuse; our God is faithful and that regardless of what we think, God is going to be there for us.

Why does God let us be tempted or put us in situations in which we are uncomfortable? The simple answer is that God does NOT put us in those situations. We put ourselves into situations where we are tempted. Temptations come in a variety of forms; we are tempted to sin, we are tempted to doubt God's mercy, and we are tempted to question our own faith. These temptations are NOT of God, but God will let us go through the temptations that Satan throws our way so that we can learn to trust God to get us through them.

Temptations surround us in our walk through this life. Many times, we do not even recognize them as temptations. I can think of so many times that temptation has assaulted me that it would take a book of those stories alone to relate even a tiny part of them. If we are honest with ourselves, we would all say the same thing.

God knows that sometimes, no matter how good our intentions that we will succumb to the temptations that assault us. How many times in our lives have we said, "I am going to lose twenty pounds!"? I have said that innumerable times; and I have started a diet with the absolute intention to stick to that diet. I have even promised God that I will lose the weight. But a week or two into the diet, a situation presents itself where I am uncomfortable with having to stay on that diet; perhaps it is at a family holiday dinner, or at a restaurant with a friend who is having a piece of pie and keeps telling me to have a piece because the pie is delicious. So, rather than have to explain that I am on the diet, I will compromise myself and order the pie, rationalizing to myself that I did it so that I would not make my friend or client feel uncomfortable ordering dessert when I did not.

Sexual temptation is perhaps the one that is the most provocative and pervasive temptation in our society today. The movies and the liberal morals of Hollywood's glamour crowd today make having sex out of wedlock or cheating on one's spouse appear to be the normal behavior in our society. When the temptation presents itself, it is difficult not to rationalize and just say "why not . . . everybody's doing it?" But that is only Satan putting those thoughts into our heads, trying to create in us the irresistible urge to give in and break God's laws. If we are not prepared to resist those temptations by being grounded in God's Word, we can give in and let ourselves be tricked into sin, which Satan absolutely relishes. In the end, we not only hurt ourselves and possibly those we love, but we break the fellowship with God.

Paul tells us that though the world may tempt us, God provides us a way out of the temptation, and He promises us that if we are tempted, we are also given a way to resist the temptation. That is because He loves us, even though we may sin over and over; we are still His creation, and His Son died on a cross to free us from the condemnation of our sins. If we repent (humble ourselves before God, ask His forgiveness, and turn away from our sin), God promises us that we can be forgiven, and our fellowship be restored with Him.

The question we need to ask is not why we are going through what we are going through, but what is the lesson that God is trying to teach us through this temptation. Everything we do in this earthly life is a lesson that we are being taught to prepare us for our heavenly home. By looking for the lesson that God is teaching us, we begin to understand that God

## Don't Be a Victim: Choose Victory!

only lets us go through the things that we need to go through to make us ready to receive our heavenly home when we all die and leave this earth. They may not be pleasant experiences, but they will benefit us if we face them with the mindset of looking for the lesson and the good that God is trying to show us as we go through them.

> Our Father, I ask that you spare me as much temptation as possible, but when I must go through a temptation or a challenge, please help me remember to look for the lesson that you are trying to teach me so that I can be a better disciple for you here on this earth, and be better prepared for the role that I am to receive when I die and come to heaven to be with you and to fellowship with you." *AMEN*

## Day 35

# Why Obey God?

*"Not everyone who says to me, 'LORD, LORD,' will enter the kingdom of heaven, but only the one who does the will of my Father who is in heaven. Many will say to me on that day, 'LORD, LORD, did we not prophesy in your name and in your name drive out demons and in your name perform many miracles?' Then I will tell them plainly, 'I never knew you. Away from me, you evildoers!'"*

MATTHEW 7:21-23 (NIV)

IN THIS VERSE, JESUS simply said that acknowledging Jesus as "LORD" (which was a common term used in Jesus' day to acknowledge people in authority over others), is not assurance of getting into Heaven. What??? Jesus has also said "I am the way, the truth, and the life; no man comes to the Father except through me. This verse of Scripture is EXTREMELY IMPORTANT!!! Why? It is because in it Jesus said that the words one speaks, while being important, are not necessarily always the true feeling that one carries in one's heart. The next couple verses clarify Jesus' meaning. *"Therefore everyone who hears these words of mine and puts them into practice is like a wise man who built his house on the rock. The rain came down, the streams rose, and the winds blew and beat against that house; yet it did not fall, because it had its foundation on the rock. But everyone who hears these words of mine and does not put them into practice is like a foolish man who built his house on sand. The rain came down, the streams rose, and the winds blew and beat against that house, and it fell with a great crash." Matthew 7:23–27 (NIV)*

In this Scripture, Jesus said that those who hear the words of Jesus and do what He says to do are wise. Those who hear and do not obey are foolish. Another Scripture says it more succinctly: *"Very truly I tell you, whoever obeys my word will never see death." John 8:51 (NIV)*. Jesus simply said this: People who obey God are showing their belief in God's Word as delivered through the prophets of old and, most importantly, through His Son Jesus Christ. People who obey God understand that God promises that His Word will never return void and that it is trustworthy. Unlike politicians and a lot of people today, we do not have to worry whether what God tells us is true, because God, being the Supreme Being and creator of everything, IS truth. His Word promises us that if we obey it, we will spend eternity in Heaven with Him. I do not know about everybody else, but that is certainly something I do not want to miss, especially after the disappointments and struggles of living in this lost world of today.

We obey God when we ask Jesus to be our personal Savior. We obey God when we read His Word, we obey Him when we follow His instructions in being baptized. We obey Him when we share the good news of our salvation with others. We obey Him when we love others and place their well-being above our own. We obey Him when we do not judge another person who says they are saved but do not act like it (we may judge their behavior, but not the validity of their salvation). All we who claim to be Christians at some time or another do not act like one!

Why obey God? He is our Heavenly Father. He created us. Are we not supposed to obey our earthly parents, our supervisors, our grandparents, and our mentors? Yes, we are. Why? It is because in each of these situations listed above, we are told to obey their instructions because they are older, wiser, more experienced in life, and are giving us guidance for our own safety and well-being. So, if we obey these earthly instructors, why would we not strive even harder to follow the instructions of our Heavenly Father who created us from nothing!

News Flash! God loves you more than you can ever imagine. He created you. He has given us, through the words of the prophets of old and the words of His only begotten Son Jesus Christ, a path into an afterlife in Heaven where there is no pain, no sorrow, no weeping no crying, and no growing old. Our God loved each one of us enough to offer all of us a pathway to eternity in Heaven through His only son Jesus. The Bible tells

## Why Obey God?

us that: *For God so loved the world that he gave his one and only Son, that whoever believes in him shall not perish but have eternal life. John 3:16 (NIV)* He also has a plan for your life; one that will give you more joy on this earth than we can ever attain by doing our own thing! *For I know the plans I have for you," declares the LORD, "plans to prosper you and not to harm you, plans to give you hope and a future. Jeremiah 29:11 (NIV) Try* as one might, nothing we plan on earth ourselves is going to give us anything better than what God has planned for us. His plan gives us something no amount of money, no toys, things, that we might accumulate can give us the satisfaction that comes through the personal, intimate relationship that is found in following and obeying God, and believing in Jesus Christ as our personal Savior. Following His plan gives us inner peace and joy that to someone who is not a Christian, cannot be explained. I can testify to that from personal experience.

In summary, there is no down-side risk by obeying God. He promises us that if we do, His plan for our lives will give us more joy, satisfaction, and contentment than anything we can comprehend or plan for ourselves. However, if we disobey Him and refuse to obey His sacrifice to accept Jesus as our Savior, we will never know what we missed, we will never know the contentment in our spirit that having Jesus as our Savior brings, and we will spend eternity in Hell separated from God and in torment after we die.

> *Heavenly Father forgive us when we fail to obey Your commandments. Help us to realize that obeying Your commandments and guidelines for living is the only real path to living life with the assurance that our path is the one that promises us the maximum joy available to us on this earth. Thank you for being the loving, benevolent, forgiving, and kind God that you are. May we always have the wisdom to seek you in all we do with all our hearts, minds, and souls. AMEN*

*Day 36*

# The Holy Spirit ... Who Is He?

"If you love me, keep my command and I will ask the Father, and he will give you another advocate to help you and be with you forever—the Spirit of truth. The world cannot accept him because it neither sees him nor knows him. But you know him, for he lives with you and will be in you. I will not leave you as orphans; I will come to you ... All this I have spoken while still with you. But the Advocate, the Holy Spirit, whom the Father will send in my name, will teach you all things and will remind you of everything I have said to you."

JOHN 14:15–18, 25 (NIV)

THE HOLY SPIRIT IS the third person of the Trinity of God. Jesus described the Holy Spirit as "He" and therefore that is how I describe Him. As such, He is no different from God the Father or from Jesus. He is always best described as God living inside of us from the moment that we accept Christ as our personal Savior and the Messiah. He is the Spirit of God living inside of us. He becomes our conscience, our teacher, and our interpreter. He is that Spirit who in those moments when we do not know how to pray, or even for what to pray, speaks to the Father for us. He knows our innermost thoughts; He knows the desires of our heart. He interprets our groanings, our indescribable joy, our pain, our sorrow, and our yearnings. When we are incapable of putting these conditions into words, He conveys them our Heavenly Father for us. He is our Advocate; He is someone who speaks on our behalf when we do not know how to verbalize in thoughts or utterances. He tells our Father what is in our hearts and conveys those thoughts, feelings, and emotions for us to the Father.

We will never see the Holy Spirit on this earth, but we can sense Him when we go through our lives. He is that small voice in our heads that creates either that uneasiness in our souls when we are sinning or about to sin, or that joy in our souls when we sense the presence and guidance of God when we are seeking Him. He is that reassurance when we are doubting ourselves and our faith. He is that sense of sorrow we feel when we sin against God. He is that sense of urgency we feel when we have sinned so that we seek the Father's forgiveness and re-establish our intimate relationship with Him. He is every good and bad feeling that will lead us back into fellowship with God. He enables that positive feeling when the relationship with the Father is re-established and in good standing.

The Holy Spirit is given almost an ethereal persona in Scripture; almost like a ghost or mystical spirit that takes possession of our bodies. Yet, when we establish our relationship with Him, we see that is not reality at all; that is not how he comes across. It is more like a part of our brain that is awakened by the needs of our spirit when we sin, when we seek Heavenly guidance, and when we just need that comforting presence to ease our fears, encourage our hearts, and be reminded of who we really are, children of the only God, the Creator, our Heavenly Father, who loves us so much that He sent His only Son, Jesus Christ, to earth to serve as the ultimate sacrifice for all our sins. He is that comforter, guidance counsellor, encourager, reminder, friend, and brother that will never leave us, try to hurt us, lie to us, use us for selfish reasons, or stop loving us, simply because He loves us in spite of our failings.

Jesus was specific when He told the disciples that He must die before the Holy Spirit is sent by the Father to indwell believers. He said that unbelievers cannot receive the Holy Spirit, cannot sense His presence, and cannot hear His guidance. Jesus said that only after He died as our sacrifice to satisfy the wrath of God for all time can His Holy Spirit be released to indwell us. Only through hearing the Word of God preached, or by reading God's Holy Word in the Bible can one even know about the existence of the Holy Spirit. But until experienced by believing in Christ as their Savior, can anyone even begin to understand that the Holy Spirit exists, and indwells us.

Why would people reject God? Why would people deny the proofs that God has given the world to see which prove to the unbiased and open-minded people of God's existence and the truth of the Bible? One of the

## Don't Be a Victim: Choose Victory!

biggest reasons today is that people have become prideful and selfish. They are too proud to believe that they cannot earn their way into heaven by being a good person, and too selfish to give up a sinful life they enjoy following a God they believe too restrictive and not fun.

It is a saddening fact that true Christians know only too well that the real spiritual, lasting joy ONLY comes through trusting Jesus as their Savior. Only then can one find the indescribable peace that comes through that relationship with Christ. Only then can one find the joy of Christian fellowship. Only then can one find the relief that comes with the knowledge his or her sins are forgiven and that he or she will spend eternity with God in a paradise called Heaven, where there is no pain, no sorrow, no tears, and no hunger. Only there can they experience the presence of the Holy Spirit with us. Only there can they experience communion with the most loving, most forgiving, most empowering, most comforting, and one-true God. Only there is hope, forgiveness, and absolution from Satan's grasp forever. Only there is where once accepted, one never wants to be anywhere else. Oh God, how I wish I could explain it better. All I can say is that I have experienced it. I have experienced being depressed to the point I wanted to die. I have experienced emotional pain that I did not think I could survive. I have experienced the disappointment of failure, loss, rejection, treachery, abandonment, and sorrow that broke me to the point where I did not think I could endure life any longer. I have experienced fear in battle that was almost debilitating. Yet, I will testify that, though still a sinner, and though still at times facing loneliness, sorrow, and all those other negative emotions, my soul is at peace. I feel loved more than I deserve, I feel blessed more than I deserve, and when I am writing this, I am encouraged, hopeful, prayerful, and feeling the joy that can only be described as sensing the presence of the Holy Spirit within me. There is the hope and inner knowledge that my God loves me and has saved me for all eternity. Nothing on earth can match the joy I feel knowing that my God, my Creator, and my Heavenly Father has loved me so much that He gave His only Son, Jesus Christ, to suffer and die on the cross of Calvary to take away the punishment and judgment of condemnation that I deserve. Instead, I will close my eyes in death someday, and at that instance, I will stand before my Savior and my God, and I will hopefully be able to bow before Him, thank Him as humbly as I know how, and hear the words "Well done, good and faithful servant." I KNOW I cannot earn that, because I am and always remain a sinner, and

## The Holy Spirit . . . Who Is He?

only through Jesus' sacrifice where He became my Savior, can I receive by grace that salvation, and for that, I truly will be eternally grateful.

> *Heavenly Father, please accept my humble apology for the sins I have committed. I confess my unworthiness to you; I confess my utter dependence upon you for the promise that, because I proclaim my belief and acceptance that Jesus is your son, and only through acceptance of Jesus as my Savior, my Messiah, and my only pathway to Heaven , can I receive the forgiveness of my sins and life eternal in Heaven with you. My soul cries out to you in gratitude and joy for Your forgiveness, and for the promise of someday coming to be with you in Heaven. Thank you, Father. I love you from the depths of my soul. Thank you, Jesus. May I someday kneel before you in humble gratitude for your sacrifice and blessings. Thank you , God, for sending the Holy Spirit to indwell me and allowing me, through His presence, to actually sense Your presence in a very real way, and experience the joy of Your presence, the grace of Your forgiveness, and the undeserved assurance of my eternal life with you through your Son, Jesus. AMEN*

*Day 37*

# Is Worshipping God Relevant in Today's World?

"Of old you laid the foundation of the earth, and the heavens are the work of your hands. They will perish, but you will remain; they will all wear out like a garment. You will change them like a robe, and they will pass away, but you are the same, and your years have no end."

PSALM 102:25–27

ASK ANY LIBERAL PROFESSOR at an Ivy League school whether they believe that God exists or not, and odds are that you will get a veritable litany of reasons that they do not believe there is a God. They will quote the so-called "facts," derived from scientists using carbon dating, that state the Earth is a couple of billion years old. They will quote Darwin's theory of evolution and hypothesize that man evolved from a single cell that somehow survived the Big Bang theory to evolve over a billion years or so into aquatic animals, then into land-based animals, and then to man. Many will scoff at the idea of a supernatural being existing where there is seemingly no physical proof of that existence.

I recently went to visit the newly built re-creation of Noah's Ark near Williamstown, Kentucky. At that museum, they tell another story. They present evidence that the science of carbon dating is very flawed. They show evidence in fossils that defy any explanation of their position and

## Is Worshipping God Relevant in Today's World?

condition other than having been part of a huge and very swift sedimentation event that would have occurred in a huge flood. They have debunked the theories of the annual circles in ice and demonstrated that in Greenland where multiple planes disappeared about fifty years ago, but the ice core samples displayed well over two hundred and fifty rings. Here is an excerpt from one of their exhibits.

> "In 1942, six P-38 fighter planes and two B-17 bombers were forced to land on the ice of Greenland. The planes were abandoned and practically forgotten. Nearly forty years later, a search was made to recover the planes, but they were not located until 1988 when advanced radar spotted them 250 feet beneath the surface.
>
> This dioarama depicts the recovery of one of the P-38 fighters. In 1992, and expedition bored a hole into the ice and received the plane piece by piece. Now known as Glacier Girl, this plane has been restored and was flown once again in 2002.
>
> The fact that these aircraft were buried under more than 250 feet of snow and ice in less than 50 years reveals the unreliability of using so-called annual layers as a dating method. The bore hole from the Lost Squadron expedition revealed far more than 50 "annual" layers because multiple layers can form every year. Observational science supports the biblical timeline and contradict popular teaching about millions of years."

For those readers interested in actual scientific and archeological evidence of the flood and creation of the earth by God, I highly recommend going to https://answersingenesis.org/, the website of "The Ark Encounter," where there is a wealth of evidence substantiating a global flood as described in Genesis, the first book of the Bible.

One can also see much of the evidence in person by visiting the Ark and the nearby Creation Museum where overwhelming evidence is presented which validates the truth of the flood and of God creating everything as described in Genesis.

These physical evidences may help someone with an open mind who is not yet a believer to see evidence that God has proved the truth of the Bible. However there really is only one way to be personally sure of the truth of the Bible and therefore the truth about God and Jesus and the Holy Spirit, and that is by believing these truths by an act of faith. Merriam Webster's definition of faith is this: "a *firm belief in something for which there is no proof* ." I and My pastor, Dr. Timothy Beougher, Assistant Dean at the Billy Graham School of Missions, Evangelism, and Ministry, and nearly

## Don't Be a Victim: Choose Victory!

a billion professed Christians around the world think this definition falls short of an accurate definition of faith.

When one looks at that definition, the term "no proof" might be accurate to a person who looks at life through the vision of someone who requires absolute concrete physical and scientifically provable fact before believing in something as real. However, for someone who is not so closed minded, the word "proof" has a much broader definition. For example, prove to me that air exists. I cannot see air, I cannot feel air, but I know it exists because every time I breath in, something moves into my lungs causing them to expand. I know it exists because if I am under water and breath out, I see bubbles form. Those bubbles have something in them, and I call that air. That is proof to me.

Likewise, when it comes to "faith," we who are followers of Jesus would argue the point vehemently that we KNOW that God is real, that Jesus is God's Son and that He died on a cross some two thousand years ago. When He did, He provided us a pathway to live eternally in Heaven with God the Father. We have multiple reassurances and written proof from the ancient texts which proclaimed the witnessing of Christ alive, the witnessing of His crucifixion, and the witnessing of His resurrection. I personally believe it because I believe every word of the Holy Scriptures are inspired by God and written down by men so that we who came after-the-fact can have testimony to confirm what we know in our very souls is truth. I came to Christ as my Savior through a child-like faith nearly six decades ago. Christ has made Himself known to me in so many ways since then so that all doubts that I may have had long ago have been crushed to dust and blown away into the winds of lessons learned.

How I pray for everyone to accept Christ as the incarnate Son of the one and only God. He is the one who died on a cross at Calvary over two thousand years to become the long promised and prophesized Messiah. How I wish for everyone to know the freedom from condemnation to hell after death. How I wish for everyone to feel the love from God, the Creator of all; I want them to feel the unbridled gratitude to God's Son Jesus Christ, who voluntarily gave Himself as a sacrifice for all mankind to provide forgiveness of our sins and reconciliation with a just and holy God.

The gift of the Holy Spirit of God, which comes to indwell each believer, reveals much about the relationship and character of God to the believer. It provides us wisdom, understanding, and guidance in how we should live our lives through reading and meditating on God's words.

## Is Worshipping God Relevant in Today's World?

Is all this relevant to today's world? God through His Old Testament prophets, and Jesus in the New Testament through his disciples and apostles testify that God is the same yesterday, today, and tomorrow. He is omnipotent (all powerful), omniscient (all knowing), and omnipresent (present everywhere at the same time). David, the psalmist, described God's omnipresence this way: *"Where can I go from your Spirit? Where can I flee from your presence? If I go up to the heavens, you are there; if I make my bed in the depths, you are there. If I rise on the wings of the dawn, if I settle on the far side of the sea, even there your hand will guide me, your right hand will hold me fast. If I say, "Surely the darkness will hide me and the light become night around me," even the darkness will not be dark to you; the night will shine like the day, for darkness is as light to you." Psalm 139:7-12 (NIV)*

In that same chapter, David described God's omniscience: *"You have searched me, LORD, and you know me. You know when I sit and when I rise; you perceive my thoughts from afar. You discern my going out and my lying down; you are familiar with all my ways. Before a word is on my tongue you, LORD, know it completely. You hem me in behind and before, and you lay your hand upon me. Such knowledge is too wonderful for me, too lofty for me to attain." Psalm 139:1-6*

In the following verses, God stated His omnipotence through his prophets in the Old Testament. Jesus stated it in the New Testament:

> Isaiah 43:13 *"Even from eternity I am He, and there is none who can deliver out of My hand; I act and who can reverse it?"*
>
> Isaiah 14:27 *"For the LORD of hosts has planned, and who can frustrate it? And as for His stretched-out hand, who can turn it back?"*
>
> Matthew 19:26 *And looking at them Jesus said to them, "With people this is impossible, but with God all things are possible."*

Reading the Bible, one will see God's supreme power demonstrated over and over. There are many instances where God destroys false gods, and the followers of those false gods. If one believes the Bible to be the true Word of God, (and I do, as I mentioned in the Introduction), then that powerful, wonderful, forgiving, loving God deserves worship. He is the One who gave His only Son to be a sacrifice for the forgiveness of all sins of every human on the planet who accept Jesus as their Savior. Worshipping Him is as relevant today as He was when He created this world, and when He saved my soul as a child.

## Don't Be a Victim: Choose Victory!

Three things will reveal the truth about God to the reader: (1) Prayer; (2) Believing in Jesus as one's personal Savior; and (3) Reading, studying, and meditating on the Word of God as delivered through the Holy Bible. Amazingly, when we accept Jesus, our eyes are opened to the plethora of evidence that is revealed to us about the existence, love, and presence of God, His Son Jesus Christ, and the indwelling of the Holy Spirit. From personal experience, I promise this is one experience no one should miss!

> Most gracious and loving Heavenly Father, thank you for opening my eyes to the truth of your Word to us humans through your inspired word, the Holy Bible. I thank you for the Holy Spirit who indwells me and intercedes with You for me. I ask you for wisdom from you that will allow me to better witness to a lost and dying world the joy of worshiping You, the only true God, creator of everything, and your son Jesus Christ. Forgive my weaknesses. Take my free will and make me a living witness for you to the world. In the precious name of Jesus, I pray. AMEN

*Day 38*

# Finding Joy and Peace through Worship

"Now to Him who is able to keep you from stumbling, and to make you stand in the presence of His glory blameless with great joy, to the only God our Savior, through Jesus Christ our LORD, be glory, majesty, dominion and authority, before all time and now and forever. Amen"

JUDE 1:24-25

"There are many who say, 'Who will show us some good? Lift up the light of your face upon us, O LORD! You have put more joy in my heart than they have when their grain and wine abound. In peace I will both lie down and sleep; for you alone, O LORD, make me dwell in safety."

PSALM 4:6-8

ONE OF THE BIGGEST complaints people have today is that they lack a sense of peace and well-being in their lives. Even though we live in the most prosperous time in the history of our world, there are still people that are looking for a sense of peace when they lay down at night and try to sleep. Our minds swirl when we close our eyes and try to sleep. Many are not able to fall asleep because of the worries of the day that besiege us. We worry about so many things, our debts, our relationships, our physical and mental wellbeing, our jobs, etc.

## Don't Be a Victim: Choose Victory!

God tells us that we can find a sense of peace and joy in our lives when we focus our attention on praising Him for the many ways that He has blessed us. The old song "Count your Blessings" rings true in our heads. Read these lyrics and take them to heart!

> "When I'm worried, And I can't sleep, I count my blessings instead of sheep,
>> And I fall asleep, Counting my blessings.
>> When my bankroll, is gettin' small, I think of when I had none at all.
>> And I fall asleep, Counting my blessings.
>> I think about a nursery, and I picture curly heads,
>> And one by one I count them, as they slumber in their beds.
>> If you're worried, and you can't sleep, just count your blessings instead of sheep, and you'll fall asleep, Counting your blessings."

Sometimes when I worry about money or debts or whatever, it helps me if I remember to stop and take a sheet of paper and just start listing all the ways that God has blessed me. As I do that, it helps put my life into perspective. I realize that I am so magnificently blessed materially and spiritually that I absolutely get ashamed of my worrying and usually fall fast asleep.

God is a wonderful, loving, generous God that created mankind to fellowship with Him. Imagine that: The Creator of the heavens and earth and all that exists wants to fellowship with us sinful humans! Why? Because He is a God of love, of generosity, and forgiveness. He loved us so much that He was willing to allow His only Son Jesus Christ to take on the form of man, then die as the ultimate and last sacrifice. Jesus' death was necessary because a righteous God will not allow sin in Haven, so a sinless sacrifice had to be provided so that all of mankind's sins could be forgiven. Jesus became that ultimate sacrifice. His death was necessary so that all mankind could be forgiven of our sins and come before a righteous and just God at our death and be ushered into Heaven for all eternity to fellowship with our Creator! That thought alone creates a sense of joy, peace, and unbelievable relief in my spirit. It can do the same for anybody that will put their faith in Christ Jesus as their Savior and seek the forgiveness of God through the blood sacrifice Jesus made for us.

I pray that everyone will try giving thanks and praising God when you are ill at ease, cannot sleep, or worried about anything. Count your

*Finding Joy and Peace through Worship*

blessings, then thank God for being the loving, forgiving, generous, healing God that He is.

> *Heavenly Father, thank you so much for being the loving, generous, forgiving God that You are. Thank you for Jesus, for providing through Him the Messiah and salvation for us sinners so that we can spend eternity with you in Heaven when we close our eyes in death on this earth. It is my prayer that whoever reads this will take advantage of Your free to us gift of eternity in Heaven with you through Jesus. It is in the Holy name of Jesus by which we pray. AMEN*

*Day 39*

# Abiding with Christ

Abide in me, and I in you. As the branch cannot bear fruit by itself, unless it abides in the vine, neither can you, unless you abide in me. I am the vine; you are the branches. Whoever abides in me and I in him, he it is that bears much fruit, for apart from me you can do nothing. If anyone does not abide in me, he is thrown away like a branch and withers; and the branches are gathered, thrown into the fire, and burned. If you abide in me, and my words abide in you, ask whatever you wish, and it will be done for you. By this my Father is glorified, that you bear much fruit and so prove to be my disciples. As the Father has loved me, so have I loved you. Abide in my love.

JOHN 15:4-9

MERRIAM WEBSTER DICTIONARY DEFINES "abide" like this: "to remain stable or fixed in a state," or "to continue in a place : sojourn ." In the Scripture above, Jesus told His disciples that to accomplish the goals that Jesus gave the Disciples after His crucifixion and resurrection, they must "abide" with Him. Jesus gave them these instructions at the last supper. He told them that He would be crucified, but after three days, resurrected. After the resurrection, Jesus explained that the disciples would spread Jesus' message to the rest of the world. In this Scripture, He explained to them that for them to be able to do what He has asked, they would need to continue to rely on Him through the Holy Spirit which would indwell them after His resurrection.

Jesus used an analogy of a grapevine to explain what he meant. A grapevine is used to grows grapes to make wine off a branch. The branch provides the strength to hold the vine, and through the branch the vine gets the nutrients needed for the grapes to grow. Jesus said he was the branch, and the disciples were the grapevine. If the disciples relied on Jesus for the strength, wisdom, and courage needed to spread His Gospel to the world, they would produce much fruit (draw many people to Jesus for their salvation). If they tried to do it on their own, they would fail. That same analogy holds true today.

God does not wish for anyone to go to Hell. For that reason, he gave the world the ultimate sacrifice, Jesus Christ, who took on the sins of the entire world. He bore the punishment for those sins so that all who accepted Him as the Messiah and God's Son, and repented of their sins, would be forgiven and would spend eternity in Heaven with Christ.

We Christians realize that we are helpless to not sin while here on earth. We realize that without the forgiveness of sin through acceptance of Christ as God's son and our Messiah, we would be going straight to torment when we closed our eyes in death. We also realize that by following Christ, we yearn to become more like Him. With the Holy Spirit living inside us, we learn to hate our sins as badly as He does, we learn to love others as he does, and we learn to forgive others so that we can be forgiven for our sins. God gave us the Bible as our roadmap for how to live. Through reading the Bible, we learn what self-less love is, we learn that we find our true happiness when we are abiding with Jesus, and we long to spend time getting to know Jesus and His Father God better so that we can serve others better. Most importantly, we learn one big truth: By following Jesus' teachings as best we can, by learning to love others like Jesus loved us with a sacrificial love, we find a source of joy like nothing else on earth can provide. I want more of that; nothing else has ever satisfied my innermost soul than abiding with Christ. I hope everyone will give Jesus their hearts and experience the joy that comes with that decision to abide with Jesus.

> *Heavenly Father, thank you for Jesus. Thank you for providing me more joy as I abide with Him than I have ever known doing anything else. I pray that you will lead me into a closer abiding with Jesus. Show me day-by-day how to better serve you by allowing me and leading me to abide with you every minute of every day. I so*

## Don't Be a Victim: Choose Victory!

*look forward to the day when I close my eyes in death and come to Heaven. I pray I have the opportunity to lay all my blessing at the feet of Jesus as I wash His feet to show how much I love and appreciate Him. I pray that I can hear what Paul said he hoped to hear "well done, good and faithful servant." AMEN*

*Day 40*

# Press On

I want to know Christ—yes, to know the power of his resurrection and participation in his sufferings, becoming like him in his death, and so, somehow, attaining to the resurrection from the dead. Not that I have already obtained all this, or have already arrived at my goal, but I press on to take hold of that for which Christ Jesus took hold of me. Brothers and sisters, I do not consider myself yet to have taken hold of it. But one thing I do: Forgetting what is behind and straining toward what is ahead, I press on toward the goal to win the prize for which God has called me heavenward in Christ Jesus."

PHILIPPIANS 3:10-14(NIV)

IN THESE SCRIPTURE VERSES, Paul told his followers in Philippi that he, who once was the ultimate Jewish Pharisee and persecutor of Christianity, had been changed by Christ, and now, his sole purpose in life was to become as much like Christ as possible, and to spread the wonderful news of Christ to the rest of the world. That would not be easy for him to do, but he said that from that point on, it was worth it.

Paul met the LORD on the road to Damascus. There the LORD struck him blind and showed him that he, who was the ultimate persecutor of the Jews, was to forget all that he was (all his training as a Pharisee and his zeal for following the Jewish law perfectly), so that he could spread the gospel of Christ to the non-Jewish world. It must have been a truly life-changing

## Don't Be a Victim: Choose Victory!

experience because Paul went from being Christianity's worst enemy to becoming its strongest advocate. Paul's thirteen letters found in the New Testament are rich with teachings that give both depth and meaning to the reality of Christ as a person and as the Messiah.

Paul, in these Scriptures told how Christ completely changed him from the old person he was to become a messenger of Christ. To those who truly invite Christ into their lives today, that same transformation takes place. Trusting Christ reveals to the believer what He has for him or her to do. Each of us has a goal that Christ chose for us before the world ever came into being. That goal is to build us up in preparation for our passage from this world to the eternal realm of God and Christ in Heaven.

It would be wonderful if Christians who give their lives to Christ could totally devote themselves to the spreading of the Gospel. Thankfully, there are many missionaries and evangelists who, once transformed, do exactly that. Most of us, however, after our transformation, still have our daily grind in life with which to deal. That grind takes our eyes off the target that Christ established for us before our birth. We encounter things day in and day out that detract us from that target from Christ. We continue to sin and continue to prioritize our worldly goals over the goals that Christ set for us.

Paul warned about that and said that, for himself, he "forgets" what is behind and "presses on" toward the goal that Christ set for him. Paul's transformation was so drastic that he was willing to give up every earthly goal and strive for the one goal that Christ set for him before he was born. Paul learned from Christ that following Him is the only way to achieve true contentment and secure that promise that Christ gives all who follow Him.

The phrase "Press On" took on a whole new meaning for me when I had one of those moments where the promise of Christ to me was made so real that I felt like the blinders were removed from me; I could see what God was saying. To achieve confidence in Christ, we must be willing totally to surrender our lives to Him. Every decision in our lives should be bounced against the gospel of Christ to determine if it is the proper one for us; we should ask if it is consistent with Christ's teachings. When we cannot be sure in our own minds, we must learn to give the issue to Christ, and ask Him to close every door but the one that we are supposed to walk through and trust that He will do so.

In my experiences since turning my life over to Him, God has been faithful. When I have failed to give Him control and made decisions on my own, they have not been necessarily bad, but certainly now looking back, I

## Press On

see where other options that I could have taken would have presented me much better results than those I made on my own.

Turning everything over to God is hard. It goes against everything that the world tells us we should do. With too few exceptions, television, the movies, and in print, we are told that we should be "an Army of one," masters of our own destiny, and in control. This Scripture and much of what I have seen since turning my life over to Christ has proven to me that these are the lies of Satan and are meant to destroy us. The choice is ours, but we are much better off when we give that choice back to God, forget our past, and let Him lead us, pressing on towards the goal that Christ set for us before time and the earth ever existed. Try God . . . He is faithful.

> Our Father, I thank You for our redemption in Christ. I thank You for the lessons in life that You have given me which teach me that real wisdom dictates my total surrender to You and the giving of my free will to You so that I can "press on" towards the goals that You have set for me before I was born. I desire you, Father; I desire to give myself totally to your leadership and the furtherance of Your kingdom here on this earth so that I might attain the redemption from my sins and entrance into Heaven once I pass from this lift into eternity.. " *AMEN*

# Conclusion

ONE OF THE GREATEST joys of my life has been the writing of this devotion. Through this process, I have experienced the joy of diving into God's Word to study His Scripture, and therein find verses that show His guidance, His support, and His will for all of us to receive His Son Jesus as our personal Savior. God wants all of us to receive Jesus as our Messiah, because He created all of us to fellowship with Him. He does not want a single soul to be lost and condemned to eternity separated from Him in Hell with Satan, his demons, and his followers.

One cannot serve two masters. We are either followers of God, or followers of Satan; it is one or the other. If we choose to reject God for whatever reason, then we will die and go to hell, forever separated from God. In the Bible, God describes the two judgments. The first judgment is the judgment for those who did not accept Christ as their Savior:

> "Then I saw a great white throne and him who was seated on it. The earth and the heavens fled from his presence, and there was no place for them. And I saw the dead, great and small, standing before the throne, and books were opened. Another book was opened, which is the book of life. The dead were judged according to what they had done as recorded in the books. The sea gave up the dead that were in it, and death and Hades gave up the dead that were in them, and each person was judged according to what they had done. Then death and Hades were thrown into the lake of fire. The lake of fire is the second death. Anyone whose name was not found written in the book of life was thrown into the lake of fire." Revelation 20:11–15 (NIV).

The second judgment is the judgment of the followers of Jesus Christ. This is not a judgment of punishment, but a judgment of the rewards we receive in Heaven based on what we did to serve the LORD while we were on earth. *"By the grace God has given me, I laid a foundation as a wise builder,*

## Conclusion

*and someone else is building on it. But each one should build with care. For no one can lay any foundation other than the one already laid, which is Jesus Christ. If anyone builds on this foundation using gold, silver, costly stones, wood, hay, or straw, their work will be shown for what it is, because the Day will bring it to light. It will be revealed with fire, and the fire will test the quality of each person's work. If what has been built survives, the builder will receive a reward. If it is burned up, the builder will suffer loss but yet will be saved—even though only as one escaping through the flames."* 1 Corinthians 3:10–15 (NIV)

I cannot imagine anything worse than having to stand before Holy God and being found not worthy of being allowed into Heaven. That would mean having to spend eternity in the burning lake of sulfur in torment and being separated from God. But God did not restrict Heaven from anyone. It is His will that every soul on earth spend eternity in Heaven with Him. But we cannot buy, earn, or deserve that privilege by anything we can do. We can ONLY receive that privilege by the act of believing in His Son, Jesus Christ, as our Savior. Period! One may not like that, may think that He is a narrow-minded God, but I see it exactly the opposite of that. I see it as a God that realized that there is no way anyone can live a sinless life in a world under Satan's influence. Therefore, the only way for one to get into Heaven and exist in the presence of his or her Creator, a righteous and just God who cannot and will not allow sin in His presence, was to provide all of mankind one ultimate sacrifice. That ultimate sacrifice must be worthy enough to cleanse all of humanity of its sins for all eternity, and that is why Jesus Christ, God's only begotten Son, came to earth and had to suffer and die on the Cross of Calvary and take on the burden of all of humanity's sins. Therefore, by believing in Jesus as the Messiah and Savior, God's wrath against sin was satisfied, and we as believers are washed clean of our sins and will enter Heaven. No one is prohibited from believing in Christ as their Savior. Likewise, no one is forced to do so. We all can choose our own destiny. Believing in Christ is an act of faith; it is a step into an unknown environment with only a promise of eternity as our motivation. But once that step is taken, then one can truly feel the presence of the Holy Spirit and the freedom of knowing our future in Heaven is secure, then and only then is the beauty and wisdom of that decision confirmed. Only then can we begin to understand why Christ was willing to be that sacrifice. Only then can the depth of the love of God for every one of us begin to be fathomed. Only then can the gratitude that every true Christian feel be understood.

## Don't Be a Victim: Choose Victory!

Only then can the peace of God that passes all understanding be felt. Only then can the guilt of our sins be washed away, and only then can we begin to love others like God loves us. I would rather never have been born than to experience life, or eternity without Christ.

It is my fervent prayer than all who read this book take that step of faith and ask Christ to be their Savior. I can tell you from personal experience that everyone who does will never look back on that decision with regrets. May God bless each one of those who read this book, as much as I have been blessed by writing it.

www.ingramcontent.com/pod-product-compliance
Lightning Source LLC
Chambersburg PA
CBHW060527090426
42735CB00011B/2410